Endorsements for
Your Success is in YOU!

For anyone at the crossroads of their career, just beginning their career, or looking for that little extra motivation to reach your next goal, this book provides the insight and advice you are seeking. Bernie captures in a straightforward and compelling way, the tips and tricks to have the career you want and deserve. Having worked with her previously, I have seen first-hand her ability to help people understand how to find their inner power and passion. As Bernie says "Your Success is in YOU!"

David Cook, Jr.
Senior Vice President & Chief Human Resources Officer

With over 20 years' experience in Career Coaching, I think this book summarizes one of the most constructive guides I have read. Bernie Frazier boils down thousands of hours of career conversations and coaching into this excellent book, and gets to the root of the core issues. She synthesizes her experience into a meaningful guide that will help any professional, whether developing 'in-place' or finding a new job. In this guide, Bernie covers the full gamut of career issues—from trust to impact of technology. This guide will be a life-long favorite of professionals dedicated to finding their voice, identifying their best-fit and creating a career that matters.

Cyd Dodson, Executive Career Coach

your SUCCESS *is in* YOU!

Empowering and Equipping You to Create Your Best Career Ever!

Bernie Frazier

GraceFive Publising

Your Success is in YOU!

Empowering and Equipping You to Create Your Best Career Ever!

Bernie Frazier, SPHR

Published by GraceFive Publishing, St. Louis, MO

Cover and Interior design: Davis Creative, DavisCreative.com

Library of Congress Control Number: 2018911035

Bernie Frazier, SPHR

Your Success is in YOU!: Empowering and Equipping You to Create Your Best Career Ever!

    978-1-7327672-0-1 (paperback)
    978-1-7327672-1-8 (ebook)
    978-1-7327672-2-5 (hard cover)

Subjects:

1. BUS012000 BUSINESS & ECONOMICS / Careers / General 2. SEL027000 SELF-HELP / Personal Growth / Success 3. SEL031000 SELF-HELP / Personal Growth / General

2018

ATTENTION CORPORATIONS, UNIVERSITIES, COLLEGES AND PROFESSIONAL ORGANIZATIONS, BOOK CLUBS: Quantity discounts are available on bulk purchases of this book for educational, gift purposes, or as premiums for increasing magazine subscriptions or renewals. Special books or book excerpts can also be created to fit specific needs. For information, please contact GraceFive Publishing Company, P.O. Box 38802, St. Louis, MO 63138 ; ph 314-482-5650; info@CAREERCompassLLC.com

To your success!

Bernie Frazier

*"I dedicate this book
to everyone
who wants more from
their career."*

Acknowledgments

Thank you, God, for Your grace, mercy, and faithfulness. It's been an interesting ride, but You've always been there guiding, protecting, and correcting me along the way.

Thank you, Mom. You have been my enduring example and supporter. I wouldn't be half the woman or half as far without your presence in my life. Your love and words of wisdom will live with me forever—"I'm a Magby, and Magbys don't quit!" I love you forever!

Thank you, John, for being the most 'significant other' I've ever had. Your love and support have been indescribable. When I've felt like I was in a storm, you've been my cover to rest my soul. You're the blessing I never knew was coming, and I thank God every day for you. I love you and I'm still showing up!

Thank you, Kim and Rolanda. There is NOTHING like having friends! Kim, you've endured my "crazy" for almost thirty years, and have still managed to provide support, accountability, and a good laugh. Rolanda, when I tried to hide, you pulled me out. You've been a great encourager, inspiration and "torch and glass" partner.

Thank you to all of my other friends and acquaintances. I've thoroughly enjoyed all of you and thank you for being a part of my life. Thank you for your support throughout the years, especially as I have walked the road from employee to entrepreneur.

Thank you to all of my former bosses, peers, and employees. Your presence and the experiences you provided me have helped me grow, and have become many of the insights I now share in my business and in this book.

Last, but surely not least, a BIG thank you to all of my current and past clients, audiences, and every organization that's given me a chance to share insights and my craft. You have challenged me to bring my best; I hope I have served you well.

CONTENTS

CHAPTER 1

It Really is in You. Trust Me

"True happiness involves the full use
of one's power and talents."
– John W. Gardner

If you've picked up this book to read it, I'm going to assume all is not well in your career, or maybe your career is going well but you want more, or you sense murky waters ahead. You've stopped in the right place! Today, so many people feel uncertain about their career and are desperate to find a way out of the black hole, but aren't sure how to do it. The good news is there is a way out, and that way is in and through YOU. You have just what you need to transform your career, whether you know it or not.

In our society, we're often taught that our answers, improvements, joy, peace, and happiness are external; what we need to accomplish our goals is outside of ourselves. We say things like, "If my employer would pay me more money, I could afford _____, then my problems would be solved," or "If I could get support from others, I would be able to do _____," or "If I could get a job like _____, my life would be so much easier." When it comes to your career, it's true that rarely will you be able to succeed by yourself; you will need help from others. However, never forget that it must always begin and end with YOU. You have the capacity needed to create the career you want, and by taking the necessary steps, it can and will be yours.

I believe we are all born with *specific* gifts and talents, that have been assigned *specifically* to us, for a *specific* reason. For many, the challenge is identifying what are those gifts and talents. Some are easy to spot—singing, painting, athletics, music—while others elude people for years. There are countless people who have gone to their graves and never known what their gifts and talents were, and how they were to be used. You don't have to be one of them. You can begin tapping into your natural abilities and interests now so you can spend the rest of your career enjoying the fruit of your efforts.

I discovered this through my own personal journey. When I realized my first job out of college was not what I wanted to spend the rest of my career doing, I became confused and frustrated because I didn't know what to do. I had over forty years left to work—what in the world was I going to do for the next forty-plus years? Of course, I could play it safe by remaining in my present career and enjoying its rewards (good salary, company car, flexibility, and freedom to manage my own day), but I knew these things wouldn't be enough to satisfy my appetite long-term. Career coaching wasn't a known option to me back then, and I wasn't aware of any other options to get assistance and figure it out. I felt trapped.

After a pep talk with myself and, admittedly, some conversations with God, I mustered up enough courage to quit my job in search of greener pastures. I landed at a new company in a different role. It was better, but still not enough to satisfy my thirst to find true fulfillment in my work. To this day, I'm not sure how I knew to take the steps I took, but I informally began implementing a plan to figure out the career path that was right for me. It didn't happen overnight, but it happened! As you read this book, you'll witness and be able to apply the same steps I followed along my journey.

It took some time to receive my "ah ha" moment, but I remember exactly when it happened. I had been on my journey for several years and working for my second employer. I was in a facilitated meeting with seventy colleagues sitting at approximately ten tables; each table had a flipchart for capturing notes. At one point during the meeting, our facilitator assigned us a question to answer at our smaller table groups. We were to record our responses and assign one person to present the table's findings to the larger group. As the most junior person at my table, I was convinced that surely one of the senior leaders would represent us. Imagine my surprise when EVERYONE nominated me to read the group's results!

When my table was called upon by the facilitator, I got up from my chair, went over to the flip chart, cleared my throat, and began to present to the larger group. When done, I went back to my seat and thought no more of it. Once every table finished presenting from their flip charts, the facilitator allowed us to take a break. As I began to walk out of the room, I noticed a lady walking toward me whom I had never seen before. She seemed so deliberate in her movement in my direction that I slowed down because it startled me. When she stopped in front of me, she struck up a conversation that went something like this:

Colleague: "Can I ask you a question?"

Me: "Sure."

Colleague: "Were you ever in Toastmasters?"

I paused before answering, because I couldn't figure out why she would ask me such a question.

Me: "No, never. Why do you ask?"

Colleague: "I was in Toastmasters for years, and the way you presented your table's information was EXACTLY how they taught us to do it in Toastmasters. You did a great job!"

Me: "Really? Well, uh, thanks. I had no idea."

Colleague: "You're welcome."

She then walked off.

I stood there for at least a minute, which seemed much longer in the moment, and was completed dumbfounded. All I could think was, "What did I say?" and "What did that mean?" For the rest of that day and several others thereafter, I wondered if there was something more I needed to understand about that exchange. Could I be a presenter? A trainer? A speaker? As I continued to ponder these questions, and my informal process, I began to see a pattern—a pattern which illuminated a talent that had been in me all along. I was a voice—a speaker! Glimpses of it had appeared throughout my life since the fifth grade, but I never recognized it. It took a willingness for me to be open to the possibilities and go on the journey of discovery for it to appear to me.

As you read this book, I invite you to begin your own journey because that's just what it is—a journey. What you'll uncover along the way certainly may lead you to your final destination. I believe you'll discover steps to move further along your path in a direction that will bring you lasting fulfillment. Even though the primary focus of this book is to help people successfully navigate their careers, the principles I share also can be applied whether you're in business, a student, or in your everyday life. No matter where you are in your journey, you're certain to experience highs and lows. Yet only those who are willing to take the journey learn how to successfully navigate the roads.

"Your Success is in YOU!" is written to help guide you along your journey. It starts by helping you understand some of the factors that may have you in a rut. It then moves you along to uncover what's inside of you, and helps you use what you already have to get what you want. Some of you probably know what your gifts and talents are, but really aren't exploring or using them. This book will assist you in finding the motivation to make whatever changes are required to achieve your goals.

For those of you still wanting to find your path, I believe this book will help you, too. When you discover your success is made up of, or at least involves, gifts and talents you already have, don't be surprised. Remember, I initially stated that *specific* gifts and talents have been assigned *specifically* to you for a *specific* reason. To give you a head start, take a look at those things you effortlessly do that bring you a lot of praise. Are you good at organizing… anything? Do people come to you when they need creative ideas? Are you everyone's "big sister" or "big brother" because you give good advice? Are you good with children? Do you find public speaking fun and exciting? As you begin to examine yourself, I think you'll be amazed by what you uncover.

Happy trails!

Questions to Ponder

1. List any skills and abilities you have displayed that others have noticed as your strengths?
2. Are you using those skills and abilities in your current career? If no, why not? If yes, how are you using them?
3. How else can you use your skills and abilities in ways they aren't currently being used?
4. What struggles do you need to overcome to experience success and fulfillment in your career?

CHAPTER 2

Armageddon in the Workplace

*"It doesn't matter what life does to you...
what are you going to do about it."*
– Les Brown

A h, the good old days…when career paths were spelled out for us! I remember the summer between my junior and senior years of college, when I interned as a sales representative for a global consumer packaged goods company. I managed my own territory and even had a company car! Everything was handed to me—the expectations, how to dress, and how to sell. I even had the opportunity to possibly work for the company after graduation. I would start as a sales representative. In eighteen to twenty-four months, I could be promoted to a district field representative. After that I could be promoted to a unit manager, and so on. The career ladder was clear and simple. Many of my friends had the same experiences in their internships or first jobs—the path was already laid out for their success within their organization. All they had to do was follow the path. The employment contract we all signed when we began working read something like this:

EMPLOYMENT CONTRACT

Dear Employee,

We are delighted that you have chosen to work for us. As an employee of the organization, we <u>promise</u> you the following:

- Employment until you retire;
- A career path, managed by us, that will give you clear guidelines for how your career will progress at every stage;
- Annual raises that range from five percent to ten percent; and
- A nice, gold watch when you retire.

Relationships between employers and employees went along like this for a while but began to change over time. People became more rushed, companies started eliminating jobs and employees, and work demands increased. On top of this, while raises, benefits, and pensions decreased, often full-time work became contract work with no benefits. The nice, smooth pace and paths to success we had come to expect started disappearing.

For most employees, the employment contract they've received over the last ten to twenty years reads something like this:

EMPLOYMENT CONTRACT

Dear Employee,

We are delighted that you have chosen to work for us. As an employee of the organization, we <u>offer</u> you the following:

- Employment for as long as you add greater and greater value, and your skills do not become obsolete;
- The opportunity to control your own destiny by managing your own career—good luck;
- Depending the kind of year we're having, raises my range from no raise to four percent;
- When you retire, let us know from where.

How did this happen? Why did things change? In my interactions with thousands of job search candidates, colleagues, and eventually career coaching clients, I began to see firsthand the negative impact these changes were having on employees. Many experienced anger, fear, stress, confusion, apathy, loss of motivation, and lack of focus. In 2013, I became curious to see if the impact I witnessed in employees merely was anecdotal, or truly a sign of the times, so I began perusing the internet for information on employee engagement.

I was pleasantly surprised when I found an article highlighting some statistics from a survey conducted by Gallup, Inc. on employee engagement, but saddened when I read some of the shocking findings from the survey. The headline stated, "Worldwide, 13% of Employees Are Engaged at Work." This survey included responses from over 225,000 employees in 141 countries around the globe. As I read this headline, naturally I did the math—this means a whopping eighty-seven percent of employees worldwide were not engaged at work. Were they serious?

As I continued to read the summary and, subsequently, pages from the actual survey results report, here are a few of the facts I uncovered. The survey categorized employee engagement levels three ways:

- **Engaged**: Employees work with passion and feel a profound connection to their company. They drive innovation and move the organization forward.
- **Not Engaged**: Employees are essentially checked out. They're sleepwalking through their workday, putting time—but not energy or passion—into their work.

- **Actively Disengaged**: Employees aren't just unhappy at work; they're busy acting out their unhappiness. Every day, these workers undermine what their engaged coworkers accomplish.
- The country with the highest level of employee engagement was Panama at thirty-seven percent. Fifty-one percent of Panamanian workers were Not Engaged while twelve percent were Actively Disengaged.
- The country with the lowest level of employee engagement was Syria at zero percent. Fifty-five percent were Not Engaged while forty-five percent were Actively Disengaged. (Considering the war and chaos taking place in Syria at the time this book is being written, these results are no surprise!)
- The employee engagement percentage for the United States was one of the highest around the globe at thirty percent. Fifty-two percent of U.S. workers were Not Engaged while eighteen percent were Actively Disengaged.

Comparatively speaking, the U.S. looked pretty good relative to most of the world's workers, but having only thirty percent of your workforce engaged at work is nothing to brag about. Consider these two points:

- The survey stated that Actively Disengaged employees costs the U.S. $450 billion to $550 billion (that's billion with a "b") each year. Remember the Actively Disengaged only represented eighteen percent of the disengaged. Can you imagine how much the fifty-two percent of Not Engaged employees costs?
- If you've ever managed or led a group of people, you can appreciate how challenging this phenomenon can be—even

when you have good employees. Now, imagine leading a group of employees where fifty-two percent of them are checked out while the final eighteen percent of them are in sabotage mode! This would be a leader's worst nightmare at work. The amount of time, energy, and expense required to try and manage this work scenario is almost unfathomable.

After reading these results, I began to ponder this current state of the workplace. What had changed that caused workers to be so disheartened at work? What caused the global economy to lose approximately $7 trillion in productivity by the end of 2017? What was causing this "Armageddon in the Workplace?" I believe two phenomena have eroded how employees view their work and work environments—technology and globalization. Let's take a closer look.

Technology.

Over the past forty-five years, the amount of technology introduced into the workplace and our everyday lives is staggering. When I was a child, it could take you over one minute to dial a person's phone number on a rotary dial phone, particularly if the number consisted of mainly larger numbers. For instance, dialing a phone number like 919-998-8798 on a rotary phone would seem to take an eternity nowadays. Today, you can dial this same number by hitting one button. If you listened to your favorite song on an eight-track, you had to cherish it, because it would be awhile before the song would come around again in the eight-track's rotation. Today, you can set up your system to play your favorite song whenever you want and for as many times as you prefer.

Technology is no longer a luxury for most people, it's a necessity. When was the last time you left your cell phone at home without panicking? How many checks have you written to pay your bills in the last six months? It's not just for young people either. My mother is eighty-four years old, at the writing of this book, and is now using her fourth computer (third laptop) and her second smart phone. She has multiple email addresses, pays her bills on-line, and will text messages and pictures to you!

Technology has not only created the work efficiency/inefficiency dynamic of today, it has caused entire industries to change. Two examples of this are:

- Uber and Lyft—Both companies have created an entirely new sub-category in the ground transportation industry called ride-sharing. Controversial since their inception, these two companies have caused a complete disruption of the taxi and rental car subcategories. In early 2018, Forbes reported results from a 2017 study conducted by Certify, a travel and entertainment expense management software company. The study and analysis were based on fifty million ground transportation receipts for 2017. Uber and Lyft accounted for sixty-eight percent of the overall receipts. Car rentals comprised twenty-five percent and taxicabs came in a dismal third place with just seven percent of receipts. Keep in mind, Uber and Lyft achieved this without owning any vehicles!

  A former client of mine is now driving for Uber and Lyft part-time and really enjoys it. He told me almost everyone he picks up states how long it's been since they've hailed a taxi—it's been years. He said his passengers always talk about how amazing it is to be able to see exactly where the driver is, how long it will take for the arrival, how clean the vehicles are, and how much cheaper it is versus taxicabs.

• Airbnb—Much like what Uber and Lyft have done to the ground transportation industry, Airbnb has taken on the established hotel and hospitality industry and is disrupting it. Founded in 2008 (then relaunched again in 2009), by 2014 Airbnb caused hotel chains to receive one-point-three percent fewer hotel nights booked, a one-point-five percent loss in revenue and three-point-seven percent loss in profits in the ten U.S. cities with the largest Airbnb presence. I have at least two personal friends who use Airbnb. They both travel a significant amount, domestically and internationally, and both swear by it. In their opinions, the prices are better than hotels and the hosts have been very kind and resourceful in helping them navigate their cities. One even confessed she'll never stay in another hotel as long as she can find an Airbnb location. Just like Uber and Lyft own no vehicles, Airbnb owns no hotels!

This doesn't mean there's anything wrong with taxis, rental cars, or hotels. It's only meant to show the impact of technology on both of these established industries, and how this impact on their businesses ultimately can have an impact on employees, their work, and work environments.

Other examples of industries shaken up by technology include retail shopping (Amazon), automobile (Tesla), news (social media—Facebook, Twitter, and others), and music (Pandora and Spotify). Technology has influenced how employees operate and experience their work in all of these industries and others.

Take a look at the following list of technological introductions to see how technology has evolved to become one of the cornerstones of our everyday lives and work:

1973 – First **handheld mobile phone** produced by Motorola

1975 – First **personal computers** introduced—the Altair 8800

1983 – First commercial public **email** service via the internet by ARPANET

1984 – First **personal digital assistant** released—the Psion (an early version of the more popular **Palm Pilot**)

1984 – First portable **digital music player** introduced by Sony

1985 – First computer-based **fax** board introduced—the GammaFax

1988 – First battery-powered **laptop** to support an internal hard disk drive introduced—the COMPAQ SLT/286

1990 – A more recognizable version of the **internet** ("network of networks") was introduced—the world wide web

1992 – First SMS **text message** sent by engineer Neil Papworth

1999 – First **music streaming** service was introduced—Napster

2000 – First device marketed as a "**smartphone**" was released—Ericsson R380 Smartphone

2008 – First **application for a mobile phone** introduced through a game called Snake on the Nokia 6110 phone

2010 – First commercially marketed **tablet computer** introduced—Apple iPad

2010 – First **ride share** goes live in San Francisco, California—Uber

My how things have changed!

Many of the devices used today in the workplace originally were thought to make working easier. By being able to send messages and information to another person in a matter of seconds, this would save a lot of time, right? Yes and no. Sending an electronic message indeed saved time when sending just one message, but as people became more efficient in their work, they began receiving more work. Instead of having an assistant take dictation for you, type up your letter and mail it, you were now expected to draft your own letters and messages and send them yourself. Workers began receiving more work, and jobs began drying up, as technology started replacing many tasks once done by humans. As jobs and employees were eliminated, work was reassigned to those employees who remained—adding more work and eliminating the very efficiencies that were once expected by using technology.

One former client recounted to me that her complete dismay with her current employer and job is a direct result of the volume of work for which she was now responsible. She had worked for the company for almost eighteen years, and really enjoyed it until the last three. Her employer went through two rounds of layoffs due to financial cutbacks, which eliminated hundreds of jobs in her division. While she felt fortunate to survive the cuts, she was now saddled with her work and that of two of her former colleagues. She went from working forty-to-forty-five hours per week, to seventy or more. After operating at this pace for over two years, she was exhausted, burned out, angry, and ready to leave for a more balanced opportunity elsewhere.

According to the Robotic Industries Association, forty percent more robots were sold in the U.S. in 2016 versus the number of robots sold in 2012. A projection from ABI Research states that by 2027, the number of industrial robots sold in the U.S. will increase almost three hundred percent. Also, according to the National Economic Research Bureau, for every new industrial robot introduced into the workforce, six jobs are eliminated. Lastly, according to the Bureau of Labor Statistics and the Bureau of Economic Analysis, from the late 1970s to the 2010s, the number

of U.S. workers engaged in manufacturing production declined
steadily. Since 2010, there have only been glimpses of increases.

Figure 2
Persons Engaged in Production in US Manufacturing, 1960–2011
(millions)

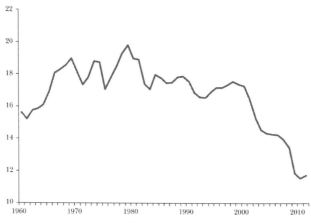

Source: Industry Accounts of the Bureau of Economic Analysis.
Note: Persons engaged in production are measured as full-time equivalent employees plus the self-employed.

During this same period, real manufacturing output in the
U.S., as measured by real value added, remained steady. Over time,
companies have been able to maintain productivity while reducing
costs and inefficiencies (whether perceived or real) by substituting
human labor with technology and robots.

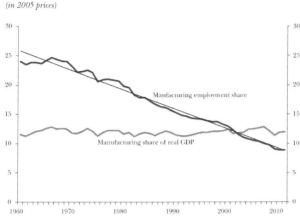

Figure 1
Manufacturing Value Added and Employment as a Share of the Total US Economy, 1960–2011
(in 2005 prices)

Source: Industry Accounts of the Bureau of Economic Analysis.
Note: Output is measured as value added in 2005 prices, and employment is reported as persons engaged in production (full-time equivalent employees plus the self-employed).

This changing dynamic is just one example of the impact of technology in the workplace—there are countless other examples that could be cited. The bottom line is this—the rise of technology in the workplace has forever changed how employees work. Employees are being required to do more work with many having the looming concern or threat of their jobs being eliminated. They're being asked to work longer hours and do more, while being promised and given less. Is there any wonder why employees are less engaged at work?

Now, let's take a look at **globalization**.

Since the days of President Theodore Roosevelt, the United States has been viewed as a major player in international trade. Today, we have over thirty signed or proposed global free trade agreements with countries and regions from around the world including Canada and Mexico to Israel to China to Kenya. Over the years, there have been arguments for and against many of these deals for various reasons, but global free trade is embedded in the fabric of our nation's DNA. We export billions of dollars of goods and services each year while importing billions. Many of the everyday goods and services we enjoy are a result of global free trade agreements including Toyotas, BMWs, Sony TVs, Samsung phones, most avocadoes, vanilla beans, and much of our oil. As a matter of fact, according to *Forbes* magazine, the top imports into the United States for 2017 were motor vehicles, oil, cell phones, and computers.

According to the U.S. Census Bureau and Bureau of Economic Analysis, in May 2018 U.S. exports were $215.3 billion while imports were $258.4 billion, creating a $39.5 billion trade deficit. Year-to-date, our deficit increased $17.9 billion or seven-point-nine percent from the same period in 2017. When our imports are higher than our exports, this can create a problem for U.S. workers—not enough global demand for our goods and services which means less work for U.S. workers.

Over the last fifty years, there's been a steady increase in imports which has severely stiffened the competition for U.S. companies. Few industries have been hit harder than the U.S. automotive industry. For the better part of seventy-six years, General Motors held the title as the world's largest automaker, but when the first quarter 2007 numbers were reported in April 2007, the world discovered that Toyota had stripped General Motors of its title. Toyota had outsold General Motors by 109,000 vehicles.

I remember when I first heard these numbers, I wasn't surprised. For years, I had been hearing about the superiority of foreign vehicles, particularly Toyota, Honda, and Nissan, over their U.S. rivals. I had heard this for so long, from so many people, that when the announcement came out about Toyota surpassing General Motors for the top spot, guess what kind of car I was driving? You guessed it, I was driving a Toyota Camry. In 2004, I had switched from an American car to a Toyota because of the numerous mechanical problems I had with the vehicle. I often joked years later that I purchased the car twice—once when I bought it and the second time in repairs!

Much of the challenge with the U.S. automotive industry began decades earlier when the public started buzzing about poor-performing vehicles with exorbitant prices. This was a great time for global automakers like Toyota, Mercedes Benz, Volkswagen, and others to push further into the U.S. market with often better-performing, less-expensive vehicles. Over time, this opened the door for other global automobile brands like Hyundai and Kia, adding even more competition for U.S. automakers.

This global competition began to erode many of the brand loyalties U.S. automakers were accustomed to having. Several years ago, I was in a conversation with my brother about this very phenomenon. I stated that I didn't think a particular division of one of the Big Three U.S. automakers would be around in a couple of decades unless they really made some drastic changes, because younger people didn't think of their cars much when considering a luxury-type vehicle purchase. He totally disagreed with me, but I then asked him one question which changed the trajectory of our conversation. I asked, *"What kind of cars do you have in your garage?"* His argument became more difficult to defend because we both knew he had a Mercedes Benz and a Jaguar. Point made!

While global free trade has opened the doors to many more purchasing options for U.S. consumers, often with cheaper prices, it also has caused U.S. companies and workers to pay a hefty price. The increased competition has put some U.S. companies out of business. Others have been forced to tighten spending while demanding more production from its employees to remain in business. The results for many employees have been in the form of job cuts, hiring freezes, elimination of pensions, reductions in medical benefits, smaller pay raises, etc.

One of the definitions of Armageddon is *"Any great and crucial conflict."* The changing dynamics of the modern workforce truly have posed a conflict for many employees (and employers). As companies have often been forced to change how they operate due to the introductions and advancements in technology and globalization, employees have been forced to operate differently. Employees have had to make changes whether they've wanted to or not. Eventually, the gap between employer demands and employee's response to those demands will have to be addressed. Until then, the battle rages on.

Questions to Ponder

1. Are you surprised to learn that only thirteen percent of the global workforce is engaged at work? Why or why not?
2. When you assess your own state of being at work, do you consider yourself to be Engaged, Not Engaged or Actively Disengaged? What has caused you to draw this conclusion?
3. Do you agree or disagree regarding the impact of technology and/or globalization on the modern-day workplace?

4. How have you seen technology impact your workplace? Your specific work?
5. Do you think technology has played more of a positive or negative role in your workplace and work?
6. Has the globalization of our economy and many workplaces impacted your work? If so, how?

CHAPTER 3

The Walls

"If there's no enemy inside,
the enemy outside can do you no harm."
– African Proverb

As discussed in the previous chapter, the changing conditions of the workplace and the new work-world order have caused many employees to become bored, burned out, and frustrated. A surprising, yet common, result of this state is stagnation. These same employees want more from their careers, and oftentimes know what they want, but fail to take action to bring about a change for the better. They can see the finish line but continue to stand where they are and watch—day after day, week after week, month after month, and year after year.

Why do people choose to remain in a state of misery when they can work in greener pastures? In my work, I've identified three primary reasons people endure the frustrations they experience at work:

1. **Imagination**—an employee conjures up circumstances in their minds that really aren't true or consistent with their past or present work experience;

2. **Self-imposed**—due to circumstances, employees make a choice to hold themselves back and not move forward; or

3. **Victim of circumstance**—external factors beyond an employee's control are creating limitations and stagnation for the employee.

These are what I call "walls." Whether real or imaginary, they are barriers people see before them which cause them to remain idle even when their present state no longer serves their good. To help you better understand, let's look at an example of each.

Imagination

Several years ago, I worked with a client named Janelle (not her real name) to help her determine what she wanted to do next in her career. She had been very successful over the previous twelve years, gaining four promotions during that time, being selected to participate on several key task forces for key initiatives, and even winning a company award for her performance. On the surface, things looked great and her future with her organization appeared to be bright. So, why was she seeking career coaching? Even though her career had been going very well, she was no longer happy and hadn't been for several years—four to be exact. Janelle had spent the last four years of her career and life being miserable. She wasn't happy at work and it was affecting her home life, because she internalized her frustrations at work and took them out on her family.

As we started Janelle's coaching program, I began to probe about why she remained in her state of misery for so long. She said things like, "I thought if I said something, I would be labeled a troublemaker," and "Since I didn't know what I wanted, I thought people would see me as a flake." My personal favorite was, "I don't know." Janelle had worked herself into such a frenzy that she was having headaches and stomach pains. She was even considering reaching out to her employer's Employee Assistance Program (EAP) because she was starting to feel like her job was in jeopardy. Maybe counseling could help "fix her," she thought.

By the end of our second session, it was clear to me that Janelle's perception of problems at work was all in her head. She had participated in a 360-degree review a couple of weeks before our first session, and received the results right before our second session. They were great! To those all around her, her work was good, her leadership of her staff was good, and she was highly respected by her peers and superiors. So, why did she remain frozen in her current job? In her mind, since she felt so miserable on the inside, she convinced herself it showed on the outside. She feared retaliation (or worse!) if she expressed her frustrations to those around her, so she did her best to keep things bottled up inside. By doing so, she conjured up an entire outcome for what would happen if she made it known that she wanted to make a change in her career. She imagined the worst.

The danger in allowing your imagination to take over is it will always take you further than you planned to go, keep you longer than you want to stay, and cost you more than you want to pay! Even if there is a semblance of truth or possibility in your circumstances, your mind will always do what my mother says, "Make a mountain out of a mole hill." When you start asking yourself, "What if....?" over and over again, chances are you've entered the imaginary zone and it's time to turn around. Becoming fixated on potential negative outcomes can affect you mentally, physically, emotionally, and spiritually. If you persist, these negative thoughts can begin to move you down a path of behavior to ultimately affect you financially, as well.

It's important to remind yourself the scenarios in your mind are just that—only in your mind. Most mental doomsday scenarios never occur. Nothing bad has happened, and there's a good chance nothing bad will happen.

As you convince yourself of this truth, you will begin to think more clearly about what you're really facing at work. Then, you'll be in a better position to address things in a way which generates a positive outcome.

Another thing to consider is the possibility that something good will happen. Imagine that! Our society, and humans in general, tend to have such a bent toward the negative when it comes to our outcomes, that we often forget things can actually turn out well! I know I've been guilty of this at times. No matter how much momentum I've had on my side, my first thoughts always focused on what could go wrong instead of what could go right. As a result, I've sabotaged my efforts and outcomes at times because of my negative thinking. To make matters worse, I could encounter someone else experiencing the same circumstance and be totally convinced that things will work out for them. Has this happened to you?

I believe people often do this to help soften the blow should things go wrong; they won't be devastated because they were prepared for it. People also don't want others to think differently about them because they're now expressing a need or deficiency (shhh, a weakness!). Also, they won't be embarrassed because they didn't set a high expectation with others who will know if things don't work out. These are just a few of the things that run counter to success.

If Janelle would've approached her situation from a more positive mindset, she would've realized sooner that her colleagues valued her and her contributions to the organization. As a result, they would've been open to listening to and helping her address her work frustrations. After all, they wanted to keep her at the company even though she now wanted to do different work. Her boss likely would've been supportive of her efforts to find work in the organization that would allow her to continue to flourish while addressing her desire to do something different. However, because she imagined scenarios that weren't likely, she spent four years being miserable at work and at home.

Self-imposed

As a client, Celeste (not her real name either) was one of my favorites. She was lively, had a great sense of humor, was open to feedback and new ideas, and did the work. After spending years in a career that brought her satisfaction, she found herself at a place in her life where she now wanted to do work that was more intrinsically rewarding. She had always wanted to work for a nonprofit organization and give back to her community using her gifts, talents, and experience. For many years, she was able to suppress this desire because she found joy in her work, but after over twenty years, most of the joy was gone. This caused her desire to pursue something new to return in a big way.

Celeste knew exactly what kind of work she wanted to do. She had even identified three to four organizations of interest. The problem was, she hadn't done anything about achieving her vision. When we started working together, I probed further into this to better understand what was going on. I could clearly see Celeste was excited when she talked about doing nonprofit work and these organizations, and flatlined when she talked about her current job. Often, the most difficult part of career development and career management is figuring out what kind of work you want to do. Since Celeste already knew exactly what she wanted, I was puzzled as to why no efforts and progress toward her career goal had occurred.

As I probed, I discovered Celeste had conducted a small amount of research which had shown that the pay for the type of role she wanted was considerably less than what she currently made. Once she found this out, she became discouraged and halted her efforts. While she didn't fully research the possibilities, she began generating reasons why the transition couldn't work. She had only begun her research and already had dismissed her entire goal! Celeste's first excuse was she didn't have time to do more research, which included connecting with people to learn more. Her next excuse was she didn't know anyone she could speak with and therefore couldn't get any additional information. Her walls were up.

If lack of time was indeed a barrier, Celeste could've reviewed her schedule to identify where time could be shaved off of her calendar to devote to this cause. I recently met a woman who has worked two full-time jobs for almost thirty years, raised three kids, made it to most of their activities, and still managed to socialize with friends semi-regularly. If she could fit all of that into her weekly schedule, Celeste could have found one or two hours per week to devote to improving her career. Others could, too.

Often, advancing a personal cause requires sacrifice and moving outside your comfort zone. In Celeste's case, networking with people she didn't know in order to gain the knowledge needed to start a new career was outside her comfort zone. As a natural introvert, the thought of this was scary, so she avoided it. Like the previous imagination example, she began to think of everything that could go wrong (but hadn't) instead of focusing on the potential positives—acquiring the needed knowledge, connecting with people who could support her efforts, meeting fabulous new people, and so on. However, by imposing walls, she delayed any forward movement in achieving her goal to create a fulfilling new career for herself. As it turned out, she already knew a few people with whom she could connect, she had just decided not to do so!

When the goal you want to achieve requires you to step outside your comfort zone, one of the best ways to address it is to remember why it's your goal in the first place. Most people are looking to make a change in their career because there's something missing—satisfaction, compensation, acknowledgement, peace of mind, stability, growth, etc. You will always run into barriers when you're trying to accomplish a goal, but if you'll remind yourself of its importance to you when the barriers show up, often this will give you the will to keep moving forward and press through.

A second thing you can do is break the actions required to achieve your goal down into smaller bites. As the saying goes, "How do you eat an elephant? One bite at a time." If you're like many, your goal is large, at least to you, so when you consider achieving it, all you can see is your colossal goal! Thinking about it too much can cause you to become intimidated which could lead you to asking yourself questions like:

- "How will I do this?"
- "Where will I get the money?"
- "Who will help me?"

By breaking your goal down into smaller steps, it becomes easier to see how you can accomplish the smaller tasks like making a phone call, sending an email, or scheduling a meeting. As you achieve the smaller tasks, you'll soon realize you've accomplished a larger effort which gets you one step closer to achieving your goal.

Victim of Circumstance

Mark's (also not his real name) circumstances were heartbreaking. Mark evolved into his career based on some natural abilities he displayed early on. A family friend needed some help in his business for a few months while one of his employees was out due to an illness. Since Mark was between jobs and could use the extra cash, he offered to help. After a few weeks, the family friend noticed that Mark was good with numbers and analysis and began to assign him larger, more complex tasks. Mark excelled. As luck would have it, when it was time for the regular employee to return, she opted to resign, and the family friend offered Mark the job full-time. The business grew and so did Mark's responsibilities. Eventually, he worked his way up to senior accountant with two junior accountants reporting to him.

A couple of years later, Mark decided to pursue job opportunities outside of his company to continue to grow his career. He landed an accounting supervisor position with a much larger organization. Things were going well until an accounting manager position opened up for which Mark applied, but was then told he couldn't be considered because he hadn't completed his bachelor's degree. Unless he went back to school, his career growth with his employer had just come to a screeching halt. Mark struggled with deciding what to do. He really liked the organization, work, and colleagues, but because of his financial obligations due to his growing family, he couldn't afford to go back to school.

Mark felt torn by his circumstances. Should he give up a good job, colleagues, and organization, or take a chance somewhere else in a larger role? Since he couldn't decide what to do, he gave in to his circumstance and remained with his employer. That is, until they announced a reorganization which threatened his job, which is what led him to career coaching.

Mark's situation is common for talented professionals who haven't completed their education, particularly those who don't have a bachelor's degree. Their talents and abilities cause them to advance, but they're suddenly stopped when they don't meet the academic requirement of the position to which they aspire. They become a victim of circumstance. Unfortunately, hitting a wall that someone else places in your way happens to everyone, but it doesn't have to stop you from pursuing a goal. If you pay attention to the news, you'll find countless examples of people who experienced a setback but found a way to overcome it to achieve their goal. If they can do it, so can you!

The bottom line is this—you'll have to deal with walls throughout your career and life whether they're walls you imagine, create, or have thrust upon you. That's just life! Some walls are small, while others are so large, they legitimately shut you down. No matter the size, there's one thing that always remains true. The great motivational speaker, Les Brown, said it best—"In life, it doesn't matter what happens to you. What are you going to do about it?" The difference between those who press past it and those who don't is a willingness to find a way. If you're finding yourself stuck behind a wall, work to identify three people in your life who can give you some **I.C.E**:

I	**Inspiration**	When you're feeling stuck, you need a cheerleader who can inspire and motivate you. This person serves as your dessert. They make you feel good about yourself and help to lift you up when you're feeling down. The person who inspires often brings a positive word at just the right moment. They can help you regain the energy and drive you need to move forward and solve problems.
C	**Challenge**	When you're feeling stuck, there's always the temptation to make excuses for why you can't get from behind the wall—they won't let me, it's too hard, I don't have time, I can't afford it, etc. The person who challenges you serves as your spinach. You may not like what they have to say, but it's usually something you need to hear. They hold you accountable and push you to do better and be better. They help you tap into deeper parts of your being—often in ways you didn't know were possible.

E	Equipment	When you're feeling stuck, this person provides you with insights, tools, and/or experiences that will help you overcome your circumstances. They are your fork, spoon, and knife. It's one thing to have someone believe in or push you, it's another to have someone give you practical advice for how to make the necessary changes. Whether the person shares tips from their personal journey, connects you with resources and people they know who can help, or is merely a wise soul that can point out critical insights, this person can give you practical advice for moving forward.

No matter your situation, if you find yourself staring into a wall when it comes to your career, know there is a way out. It may take a week, a month, a year, or longer to move past it, but one thing is for sure—if you do nothing, nothing will change. For most of you reading this, the rest of your career is a long time to remain in a work condition that doesn't fulfill your needs, so start chipping away at that wall today.

Questions to Ponder

1. How would you rate your current feelings about your career with 5 = It's Terrific and 1 = It's Horrible?
2. If your rating is three or less, how long have you felt this way?
3. For the time you've been in your current state, would you say most of what has stopped you from making changes are

really imaginary, self-imposed, or have you been a victim of circumstances?

4. Who can you turn to when you need I (Inspiration)?

5. Who can you turn to when you need C (Challenge)?

6. Who can you turn to when you need E (Equipment)?

CHAPTER 4

Developing Your Hunger

*"When you deny the world your gifts and talents,
you cause other people hardship."*
– Pastor Allen Landry

The first part of the last sentence of the previous chapter reads, *"For most of you reading this, the rest of your career is a long time to remain in a work condition that doesn't fulfill your needs... "* If I had to guess, I would assume the majority of the people reading this book fall between the ages of twenty-eight to forty-eight. If this is true, this means the majority of you will work another eighteen to forty-two years, if you work until full retirement as defined by the U.S. Social Security Administration. If you're feeling bored, burned out, or frustrated about your current work or work environment, yet are doing nothing about it, eighteen to forty-two years is a long time to remain in this state.

I want you to pause right where you are and take two to three minutes to really think about remaining in your current state for all of these years. How does it feel? What may have changed around you while you did nothing? What possibly could you have missed out on because you made no changes? For those who may look up to you, what lessons did you teach them about how to manage their career? I had a client once who jokingly stated, "Yeah, I think

I've taught my kids how to be as scared as I am about making changes." If you have kids, is this a lesson you want to pass along to them?

"Bernie, what you're saying makes perfect sense to me, but I've told myself this time and time again, and I still can't seem to find the motivation I need to do something about my current situation. What do I do?"

What may be missing is your hunger. You may not be hungry enough to make a change. You want to do more or something different. Yet, when you realize it will take effort (maybe lots of it!), and possibly coming out of your comfort zone, suddenly your desire has waned and you convince yourself that your current situation really isn't that bad. The hours you work really aren't that long after all. Your boss isn't that bad, and the job may be leading to nowhere but that's okay, it's a steady paycheck and benefits so you can *tolerate* it. Besides, you don't have time to add other things to your plate anyway, right?

Let me share some insight with you about tolerance. Several years ago, I was asked to serve as a co-facilitator for a company-wide leadership class. This class included an enlightening exercise about attitudes toward differences. The exercise outlined a Tolerance Scale, co-developed by Global Novations and my employer, which consisted of ways people react to individuals they perceive are different than themselves. While this exercise dealt with diversity and inclusion, I believe you'll understand and appreciate how the Tolerance Scale shows us what tolerating people and issues in our lives really means.

There were five ratings for the Scale, but the one that struck me the most was the definition for tolerance. The summarized version is *putting up with someone or something. If you had your choice in the matter, you wouldn't have them in your space.* Do you notice anything out of the ordinary about this definition of tolerance? The first time I saw it, I sure did. Did you view tolerating people, events, or things as an noble quality to possess? Did you consider it a sign of strength? A sign of getting along; being politically correct? When I read this, I went into panic mode trying to remember people I had tolerated in the past, and the impact my tolerance behavior may have had on them.

Now, compare and contrast this to your current career circumstances. If you're merely "tolerating" where you are, how does tolerating your circumstances now look to you? Is this a good place? Probably not. If you had your choice, most likely you would be somewhere different or doing something different. I believe the longer you allow this state to persist, the worse it can become. You may wake up one day and realize your current career state repulses you!

The good news is you do have choices. Those choices may not be easy to make, but they're still available to you if you're hungry enough to go after them. Yet, at the end of the day, nothing, and no one, can cause you to choose the changes you need for a better career—only you can do this. The old saying, "If it's going to be, it's up to me" never rang truer than right here, right now. This is your career—no one else's. No matter how much people love and care about you, no matter how invested others are in your success, until YOU choose to make a change, nothing will change—at least, none of the changes made will stick. I know this because I've been there.

I began my business in 2011 with tremendous excitement. I had been doing career coaching and speaking for years, but finally decided to become official and launch my business,

CAREERCompass, LLC. I was still working a full-time job, so I could only focus on it in the evenings and on weekends. However, over time, I began to see the business grow and my name recognition was increasing in my local market. It was exciting and I was loving it.

After almost four years, I decided to take a chance and strike out on my own. I quit my six-figure job to exclusively pursue my business. I knew it was a big gamble, but I have always been a bit of a risk-taker so I wasn't overly scared to step out. I had also made a promise to myself that I wouldn't allow my eightieth birthday to pass while harboring regrets for things I didn't at least try.

I was excited at first, but things quickly changed. Suddenly, I couldn't find my way. I couldn't figure out where to focus my efforts, and opportunities that looked very promising before I quit my job seemed to dry up. The more time passed, the more frustrated I became with my situation… and myself. I began to feel like a failure, and this wreaked havoc on my confidence. I was telling clients and audiences all they could and should do while feeling like a loser inside! I felt like a fraud. Most people didn't know, and those who did tried their best to encourage me, but it was useless. After a couple of years, I quit trying. I decided to check out for a while and let the business go where it would go. Even though a few opportunities and clients continued to come my way, I did very little to capitalize on them. I was bored, burned out, and frustrated!

After a few months, I realized the desire to do more was still there—it had been set aside, not buried like I thought. Initially, I had no idea of what to do with this new revelation, but was very happy to know the desire wasn't gone. While I knew I would have to do something, I still didn't seem to have enough internal drive to actually make changes. My challenge became creating enough hunger within myself to do something about it. It wasn't easy and took some time, but I implemented four steps to help refuel my drive. I'm sharing them to help fuel your hunger and drive you to action. I believe if you can find the right motivation, the changes you need to make will quickly happen and your results will be amazing.

How long? The first thing I did was exactly what I outlined on the previous pages—I took a long look at my circumstances, which I was tolerating, and asked myself three questions:
- "If nothing changed with my circumstances, would this be enough for me?"
- "How long could I continue in this manner?"
- "If I wanted better, what was I willing to do to get it?"

As I pondered these questions, my answers became clearer—my present state wouldn't be enough, I couldn't go on like that much longer, and it was time for me to do something—no more excuses.

When you ask yourself these questions, I encourage you to be totally honest and write down your answers. Since no one knows you're doing this exercise, you don't have to worry about their opinions of your answers. Further, being dishonest with yourself won't help you. If you don't believe your responses are what you want them to be, this is still no reason to be dishonest with yourself. How you feel is how you feel and your reasons are your reasons. Attempting to mask them to yourself won't change them. As the Bible states, "…..the truth will make you free."

If you aren't really ready to make changes, don't try to convince yourself on paper that you are—this is a head and heart thing, not a 'write it on paper' thing! Instead, further explore *why* you're not ready. Is there something only in your imagination that's holding you back? Have you imposed a barrier on yourself which is causing a delay? Has another person or an external force created a situation that's preventing you from moving forward? Whatever the reason, use what you discover to begin refueling your hunger for more.

Self-compassion: If you answer the three questions and discover it's now time for a change, you may begin to feel despondent because of the time you think you've wasted by doing nothing. This is what happened to me. I began counting the months and years I felt I wasted being confused, feeling sorry for myself, and shutting down. It became a form of grief—I was grieving the time I felt I had lost.

For a while, this grief sabotaged my hunger for change. I began to focus more on the time I lost instead of the great opportunities which were ahead of me and all of the things I wanted to do. My imagination began to take over, and I started saying to myself, "I can't do this," and "It's too late." This caused me to once again make choices that slowed down progress. If this happens to you, you must recognize what's happening and stop this thought process!

The best way to address self-defeating thoughts is with the second step, self-compassion. Give yourself a break. Negatively speaking to yourself and dwelling on the "what if," "what should've been," and "what could've been" moments is counterproductive and actually can take a toll on your mind and body. According to an article written in *Psychology Today*, our brains have a negativity bias.

Negative information has a natural tendency to stay with us longer than positive information. We are wired to be more sensitive to negative news. Therefore, the more negative news we feed ourselves about ourselves, the more likely we are to internalize it as true—even if it's not. Over time, this negative "food" will begin to affect your mental and physical health just like other forms of abuse.

Instead, remind yourself that regardless of the outcomes, you made the best decisions in the moment with what you knew and what you had. Isn't this true most of the time when it comes to decisions for yourself? Rarely have most people made a conscious decision to sabotage their efforts and make things more difficult and frustrating for themselves. Even if a person does this, it's usually for a good reason—at least to them at that time. I'm sure you're the same way. Whether you've made good or bad choices, weren't you at least trying to get to a better end? No one makes perfect choices every time, not even you, so give yourself a break.

Further, instead of focusing on the negatives, make a conscious effort to shift your thinking to focus on the positives:

- Your fire is back!

- You're now excited about your future!
- You have the power to change your circumstances!
- Your circumstances will change!

Now that's positive news!

You may be thinking, "I've heard all of this positive thinking stuff before and it didn't work." If this is you, my question to you is, "How often or how long did you focus on transforming your thinking?" You must understand, this is not an overnight process. Many remain stuck in a pattern of negative self-talk for years, even decades. If it has taken you decades to become proficient in your negative thinking, it's highly unrealistic that you will root it out within a few days, weeks, or months. It's an ongoing, lifelong process for which you must always remain vigilant. If you commit to the process, you'll reap the rewards. Don't give up!

To understand the power of transforming your thinking, the next time you catch yourself in a negative thought pattern, consider how you feel mentally, physically, and emotionally. You may feel lethargic, sad, hopeless, scared, confused, or insecure. When you become aware of what you've just done to yourself, make a conscious effort to turn that same thinking around to positive thoughts. Also, begin to speak positive words out loud. By doing this, you help to drown out the negative thinking. When accomplished, examine how you feel—energetic, creative, empowered, happy, and free? Which do you prefer—the results of negative or positive thinking?

Why? I think humans are truly fascinating beings. Although we are inherently selfish, we also have an internal drive to do something beyond ourselves—to serve. How can we be selfish and service-oriented at the same time? For me, this is one of life's perplexing contradictions. Many people work hard to achieve great success, fortune, and fame, yet feel unfulfilled when they get it. However, no matter the level of success, I believe every person reaches a point in their life when they ask the question, "Why am I here?"—code for, "Who am I here to serve and in what capacity?"

If you'll recall, in Chapter One I stated, "I believe we are all born with *specific* gifts and talents that have been assigned *specifically* to us for a *specific* reason." I truly believe this. Your gifts and talents didn't randomly land on you. They were given to you to address certain needs and solve certain problems for certain people or groups. Unless you take the time and put forth the effort to find out why, you may never know and neither will your audience. "My audience?" Yes, your audience. Your audience may only be one person or it may be millions, but there's someone out in the world that's in need of what you can offer.

The quote at the beginning of this chapter is one I heard in a sermon that was preached at my home church in the late 1990s by a guest pastor, Allen Landry. I remember enjoying his message, but the only part of his teaching I can recall is this quote—"When you deny the world your gifts and talents, you cause other people hardship." I remember it because it shook me to my core. At the same time, *I* was in the process of trying to answer, "Why am I here?" The thought of people suffering because I wasn't fully utilizing my gifts and talents really hurt me. I kept imagining people being lost, fearful, and crying because I wasn't doing what I was supposed to do. That moment fueled my hunger.

I urge you to ask yourself who might be struggling or hurting if you aren't fully utilizing your gifts and talents.

I spent almost four years of my career working in a pediatric hospital. I honestly can say I had never worked in a place where I encountered more people who truly believed they were doing the work they were supposed to do. It was wonderful to experience. In my first month, I met with different leaders throughout the hospital to begin making connections, explaining my work, and gaining an understanding of their areas and needs from my team and me.

During one of my first meetings, with the director of the Neonatal Intensive Care Unit (NICU), she asked if I had ever had been in a NICU ward. "No, I haven't," I responded. She then asked if I wanted to see it. I replied, "Absolutely!" so off we went. Seeing such tiny babies completely amazed me, yet I knew I could never do that work. As we were completing my tour, I was introduced to one of the staff nurses. She had worked with the babies in the NICU for twenty-eight years. I asked her how she could do this work and for so long. She replied, "These are my babies. I can't imagine working anywhere else." She had a *specific* talent to work with a *specific* group to help them and their families work through a *specific* hardship. She was right where she was supposed to be, and those babies and their families tremendously benefitted from her loving care. She was rewarded everyday through her service to her patients.

The gifts and talents you have were not given to you to serve *you*. Whether it's working with numbers, caring for sick children, keeping others organized, selling goods and services, or running your own business—you received these to address a need or solve someone else's problem. Have you ever wondered why others marvel at how you're able to almost effortlessly do something they can't fathom accomplishing? When people compliment you regarding what you do, do you shrug it off because you don't see it being a big deal? It's easy, right? Have you ever marveled at things others could easily do that would leave you frustrated, and watched them shrug it off when you complimented them? Do you see how this works? Your gifts are not for you, they're for others, which is why they recognize them and you often don't.

Four years, three months, and thirteen days after I launched my business, I experienced the most powerful example of why I had to do the work I felt most utilized my gifts and talents. Approximately six months prior to this date, Angela (not her real name), a friend since childhood, reached out to me for career coaching assistance. She lost her job, fell on difficult financial times, and had been unsuccessful in finding a new job. I agreed to work with her and we spent several sessions revising her resume and discussing interviewing and networking techniques, among other job search topics. When we were done, I wished her good luck and told her to let me know if she needed any other help.

Almost six months later and exactly five days before I was scheduled to facilitate an all-day training session for a group of up-and-coming leaders, I was working on my facilitation notes while my frustration grew with each passing minute. For two weeks, I had been struggling with one portion of my notes. I needed to present a segment on "Why are you (here)?" and although I had generated several ideas, none resonated with me the way I desired. I was getting nervous because it was my first time working with this group and I really wanted to make a great impression. On the same day, I received a call from Angela. She wanted to know if I was busy and if not, could she come by because she wanted to share something with me. I gave her a time when I would be available and told her to come by. When she arrived, I greeted her, we talked, laughed, and caught up on old times and the latest happenings. Suddenly, she shifted the conversation and became more serious.

Angela—"I guess you're wondering why I wanted to come by today?"

Me—"I was a little curious but it's no big deal."

Angela—"I want to thank you."

Me—"Thank me for what?"

Angela—"You helped save my life."

Me—"What? How? What did I do?"

Angela—"Because you helped me with my resume and interviewing and stuff, I was able to find a job—a job with good benefits. A couple of months later, I found out I had congestive heart disease. Because you helped me find a job with benefits, I'm now able to work with one of the best cardiologists in the city. If I didn't have this insurance, I could be dead right now. So, thank you."

Can you imagine how completely stunned I was? I literally sat in place and stared at her because I couldn't believe what she just told me. My friend for thirty-five years had just told me the gifts and talents I chose to use led to a short series of events that may have saved her life! I then stood up to say something but could only cry. Never in my wildest dreams would I have thought the work I did to help people with their careers could possibly help save a life. Never. I had my example for my facilitation session.

When you begin to do the work that calls on your talents, and you truly enjoy it, you never know who you'll end up serving and what impact you may have—therefore, serve well and serve often.

Don't do it alone. Throughout U.S. history, we find countless examples of people accomplishing things on their own and being heralded for it. When you think of the Underground Railroad, you immediately think of Harriet Tubman. From 1850 to 1860, Harriet made nineteen trips and rescued over 300 slaves from the oppression of southern slavery. Evel Knievel was regarded as the most popular motorcycle stunt performer in history. With his jaw-dropping jumps and unusual name, he was known all over the world for his amazing talent and work. There was even a hit television show from 1949-1957 which played to the notion of working alone—The Lone Ranger. He was the lone survivor in a patrol of six Texas rangers who had been attacked. They had traveled throughout Texas and the American West to assist those under attack by criminals. The show was so popular that you can periodically still find the episodes showing in syndication.

There's just one flaw in this thinking—none of the three listed above worked alone. Harriet Tubman was helped by hundreds, maybe thousands, of Abolitionists across the southern and northern States who hid runaway slaves from their would-be captors. Evel Knievel hired and worked with a crew of performers, stunt coordinators, and other personnel in the planning and execution of his jumps. The Lone Ranger had his trusted sidekick, Tonto. Even the creators of a television show were wise enough to realize the star couldn't succeed alone.

While you may want to be the hero in your own story, don't waste precious time and energy on activities that aren't as important. Remember, it's achieving the goal that counts, not the number of people who help you along the way. As your hunger grows, begin creating a list of people from whom you might need help.

Whether it's people who can give you I.C.E. (Inspiration, Challenge, Equipment) or fulfill another need, write them down and begin determining what specific help you may need from them.

You may also need to put your ego aside. Too many people (including yours truly) have a difficult time asking for help. Whether it's because you think asking is a sign of weakness, you feel like you'd be burdening others with your struggles, or are embarrassed because you can't do it on your own, if others who know and care about you have the capacity to help, at least ask. If this same people needed help and came to you, I'm sure you would be more than willing to help. So, why would they not want to help you in return? Don't delay your breakthrough, solution, or success because your ego is larger than your need.

"When you deny the world your gifts and talents, you cause other people hardship." Thank you, Pastor Landry, for sharing this important message.

Questions to Ponder

1. Are you *tolerating* your current career state? If so, why?
2. Are you *really* ready to make a change in your career? If yes, how do you know for sure? If not, what's holding you back?
3. Have you been beating yourself up over your current career state? What will you do to turn your negative talk into positive talk?
4. Does Pastor Allen Landry's quote resonate with you? Why or why not?
5. What is your personal response to the question, "Why are you here?"
6. Who's help might you need to reignite your hunger?

CHAPTER 5

The One Question You Must Ask and Answer

"When values are clear, decisions are easy."
– Roy Disney

In chapter two, I discussed the employee engagement work done by Gallup, Inc. and the shocking results from their global survey. With an almost seventy percent rate for employee *dis*engagement in the U.S., is there a solution that can improve this challenge for employees and employers? There is, and I believe a big part of it lies in employees' ability to answer one question—**what do you want**? It sounds simple, but is it?

To date, I've spent almost thirty years interacting with job seekers, coaching clients, and speaking before audiences. As I reflect back on the thousands of people I've interviewed, coached, educated, and encouraged, there's one element that has been the most consistent—most people don't know what they want to do. Again, it sounds simple, but it's not. Over the course of time, I have incorporated this question more frequently into my work and personal conversations. When I ask the question, "What do you want?" the overwhelming majority of people can't answer it. Instead, they answer one of the following four questions:

What do you do?

What have you done?

What do you think you can do?

What have other people told you to do?

The problem with these responses is none of them answers my question.

What do you do? Telling me what you do can be very different from what you *want* to do, and is often the case. There are millions of people doing things, but far fewer are doing things they *want* to do. What you do is current state, while what you *want* to do is future state. What you do doesn't require you to make any changes or put forth any extra effort. What you *want* to do may require you to conduct a complete overhaul of your career. What you do helps to show others you're busy—you have a lot going on—but it doesn't show that you're productive when it comes to effectively managing your career. You're on the hamster wheel, but you're not moving forward!

What have you done? If you respond to the question, what do you want, by providing details of things you've already done, you're also missing the mark. Stating what you've already done is past-tense, not future-tense like the question I asked. This gives you a great opportunity to share your past accomplishments, but it doesn't begin to speak to what you want to accomplish in the next chapter(s) of your career. I believe people resort to this type of response because they're hoping it will provide others (and themselves!) an understanding of their *ability* to be productive and successful in the future. They've been successful in the past so, of course, they'll be successful in the future. When you respond to the question with what you've done versus what you want to do, it can also create a false sense of security. It may help you convince yourself that everything is okay—you have it under control because of your successful track record—when you know, deep down inside, you're not being fulfilled.

What do you think you can do? The most common response I get when I ask, what do you want, is what people *think* they can do. "I think I can do…," "I'm thinking about trying…," or "I could do…" Again, this avoids answering the real question. When you respond with what you think you can do or have, you're saying you don't know what you want or you don't believe you can really have it. When you don't know what you want, you come up with a list of things that are possible, hoping one of them will get you to an acceptable response. Saying "I think…" is like using a hook and bait in fishing. You throw it out, hoping it will catch something worthwhile. When you take this approach, you're leaving your career future to chance. For many, this has been their approach, which explains why so many people are disengaged at work.

When you don't believe you can have what you want, you're telling the world you lack confidence in yourself or your ability to change your circumstances. This is common. Whether it's conditioning through the words and actions of others, or through your past attempts to try something and it didn't work, you now may have limitations (walls) in your thinking which cause you to question yourself. I understand this one well. In my earlier attempts to do things in my business, my confidence began to dwindle when I didn't receive the types of responses I wanted or felt I should've received. It caused me to become very hesitant about things I might want to try—I heard myself saying, "I think…" more often than I cared to hear. My fledgling confidence even delayed to start of me writing this book by a couple of years!

What have other people told you to do? I've had people respond to the question, what do you want, by telling me what others have told them to do. There are so many examples of people in our society who end up choosing careers because their parents wanted them to have a certain occupation, or it runs in the family. Others choose a career because people have told them they should do it, and these are people they trust and respect, so why not do it? The problem with this approach is you end up selecting a career that works for others but not for you—the person who actually will have to do the work. While it's understandable to not want to disappoint your family or disregard the recommendations of those you trust and respect, it's critical for you to remember that it's your career! If you choose a career or work environment that doesn't work for you, you are the primary person who will suffer for it.

So many who struggle with this question do so because they haven't thought about their wants for so long they no longer know what they want. They may have known years ago, but life (work, family, bills, religious duties, vacation, illness, travel, volunteer work, and household chores) got in the way and choked out their wants. Life slowly crept in and took over their time, activities, finances, and thoughts, until there was no room left for what they wanted.

Also, some people think it's selfish to declare what they want. We live in a society where the word selfish is rarely, if ever, considered a positive thing. Being selfish means you aren't considering other people. In a society where giving to others is highly regarded, considering yourself first, or only, loses the argument almost every time. This is especially true for women who often are praised for making sacrifices for others, especially their families. So, hearing, "What do you *want?*" can cause a tug-of-war in your brain. Answering this question doesn't allow you to continue being a "good person" in your mind, but not answering the question keeps you in a state of career frustration. So, what do you do? In order to be able to press past any internal blocks, you must shift your thinking and begin to see the good in focusing on what you want. For instance,

- You are courageous when you stand against the norm and identify a path that will bring you lasting fulfillment.
- You're helping others when you model how to identify your heart's desire.
- By focusing on what you want, you'll be able to help those who are in need of what you have to offer.

Do you see how small shifts in your thinking can make a big difference?

"What do you want?" is the most important career question you can ask, and the least answered. It is the foundation of your decisions and actions. If you don't know what you want, how do you know who can help you? How do you know who you need to know within your company, what education/training you need, or what internal jobs to pursue? How do you know if the right opportunity is available in your company or if you need to seek opportunities elsewhere? If pursuing new, external opportunities, how do you determine how to structure your resume, what jobs to target, with whom you need to network, or how to prepare for your interviews? You don't.

I had a client who wrestled with this dilemma but initially didn't realize it. When we began working together, he was very angry with his current employer because he felt he was being denied opportunities for learning and growth. By our second session, he presented the letter of resignation to me he was prepared to give to his supervisor. In order to slow him down to ensure he was considering all possibilities, I asked him what he wanted to do once he left—he couldn't answer. "So, you mean you're going to quit your job, with no current prospects for another, to pursue a job for which you don't know what you want?" He looked sheepishly at me and said, "I guess that does sound crazy, huh?"

By the end of our session, he decided not to quit his job. In our next session, we began working through a process to help him discover what he wanted to do. Guess what? What he uncovered was a career path that was available within his current company! He was going to walk away from almost fifteen years of time invested with his employer when what he wanted was right under his nose—all he had to do was figure out what he wanted. By the way, several months after implementing the plan we created, he was promoted!

I spent many years working in Corporate America. During that time, I witnessed many concepts, phrases, and buzzwords come and go. Remember when Total Quality Management (TQM) was all the rage? Suddenly, TQM was out and LEAN and Six Sigma were in. Synergy was huge in the 1990s, but I haven't heard this word used in years. At one company I worked for, we even played a game called Corporate Bingo. This involved marking a spot on the game board when someone used one of the popular corporate buzzwords or phrases listed; we marked a lot. Some of today's popular buzzwords and phrases are human capital, wellness, knowledge management, stakeholder, and my favorite, collaboration. Let's see how long they remain in vogue!

One word which has never gone out of style is strategy (or strategic). People still love to be able to tell others their work is very strategic, or they work on the strategic business development team, or they're a member of the strategic planning committee. To many, there's something powerful and sexy about being able to use the word strategic when describing the work they do. I've had clients and audience members brag about the depth of strategy in their work. Yet, when I ask these same strategic employees to tell me about their career strategy, I receive blank stares. Does this sound familiar? If this describes you, I have a question for you:

How can you be so strategic about someone else's business, yet so tactical about your own business?

My own business? Yes, your business. Unless you purchase a business license, conduct a fictitious name search, establish your articles of organization, and obtain a federal employer identification number, you are not considered a business owner (at least by governmental standards!). Therefore, your career is your business, and the name of your business is YOU, Inc. This is how you spend your days, where put your effort, how you generate income, and to whom the government will contact to determine the taxes you're required to pay. You are not an employee in your career—you're the owner. The goals, decisions, and actions required to get what you want must be determined and executed by you. If you aren't approaching your career in this manner, this may explain any dissatisfaction you're experiencing.

If you could witness your employer's top executives during an annual planning meeting, what do you think you'd see? Would they be sitting around waiting to see what others were going to do to affect the business they were in charge of running, or would they use information they've obtained to decide where they want the business to go in order to achieve specific goals? Would they take a, "Well, let's just see what's going to happen" approach? This isn't likely because they're aware of the fact that they run a business. Yet, too many of you (employees) are reactive when it comes to your career—you wait to see what your employers are going to do to decide your next move. Instead, you should be determining what you want, then working with and through your employer to get it. If you wait on your employer to do all of the goal setting and execution, they'll most likely establish an internal current that works for the organization, leaving you empty-handed. Your goal should be mutually beneficial for your employer and you, but if you aren't deliberate in making this happen, you'll lose out every time.

Most of this chapter has focused on asking what do you want? Yet, there's another part that's just as important and that's *answering* this question. Asking the question is easy; answering it often isn't. If you don't currently have a clear and concise response, it's important to spend some quality time thinking about it. It's also important to not make any important career decisions until you do. Without having an answer, how do you know if a lateral move is really a good move for you to make? Is the promotion really good for your career because you'll have a bigger title and make ten thousand dollars more per year?

When I left Corporate America, I worked at the manager level. In the years leading up to my departure, I had opportunities I could've pursued and exploited to be developed and considered for a promotion to a director-level assignment. However, I never pursued them because I knew what I wanted. I knew my goal was to eventually leave my corporate career to pursue my own business. I knew I would need to work full-time for a period of time in order to generate momentum and determine whether I could do it or not. I also knew moving up the corporate ladder would require more of a commitment and longer hours on my part—time I wouldn't have to map out, launch, and grow my business. While my choice may have seemed unorthodox to others, it made perfect sense to me. Because I knew what I wanted, I was able to make moves to help me achieve my goals, not meet their expectations.

What do you want? That's the question. What's your answer?

Questions to Ponder

1. Why is it important to ask *and answer* the question, "What do you want?"

2. Are you able to answer this question for yourself? If yes, what do you want? If no, why not?

3. What steps have you taken, in the past, to align your present career to what it is you want to do?

4. "What do you want?" sounds like a simple question, but why do you think so many have struggled to answer it?

5. What is your career strategy?

CHAPTER 6

Finding Your Bullseye

"Judge a man by his questions rather than his answers."
– Voltaire

By now I hope you understand how critical it is to know what you *want* to do in your career; to find your bullseye. Knowing what you want is indeed the foundation from which everything else should be built. Without having an answer to this question, your career choices and moves will be nothing more than shots in the dark. You may wake up one day and realize your career is nowhere near where you want it to be, because you made moves based upon factors that weren't consistent with what you really wanted. You used these factors to make decisions because you didn't consider one very important question—what do you want? Or, at one time, you knew what you wanted but, again, allowed other factors to lure you away.

For instance, while conducting a talk several years ago for the local chapter of a national human resources association, one of my key points circled around the question—what do you want? As I spoke more on this point, a young man sitting in the front row began to give me a, "This is bull crap!" look. A couple of minutes later, he raised his hand to ask me a question. He stated, "I hear what you're saying, but I don't agree. I was a finance major and began my career in this field. After a couple of years, my boss approached me about a job opportunity he thought would be great for me in Human Resources. It sounded pretty cool, so I took it. Now it's been five years and I'm in Human Resources, but I really want to work in Finance. So, just because you know what you want doesn't mean you're always going to get it."

I couldn't wait to respond to him. My response went something like this, "You raise a good point, but let me ask you a couple of questions. When your boss approached you about the job opportunity in Human Resources, did he also put a Glock to your temple and make you take the position? Or, did he offer you a salary increase and nicer job title?" When I finished my questions, I noticed a sheepish look began to appear on his face. He knew I was right. Instead of remaining true to what he wanted, he allowed someone else to tell him what he *should* want, and he abandoned the finance ship. He fell for the oldest trick in work history—more money! He failed to ask himself the right question.

If you've ever done this, don't feel bad. Many people have moved off course with their career because of money or other factors that end up not being enough to sustain their satisfaction. When this happens, the key is finding what you now want and pursuing it. If you're still struggling to identify what you want for your career, this chapter will help you. It's what I and many others have done to help us piece together the puzzle of career fulfillment.

The focus of this chapter is a series of questions for you to answer. This is not a reading chapter, it's a working chapter. Often, by taking a long look at yourself—your habits, past activities, interests, and influences, you can discover hidden talents and interests. I encourage you to do the following for each question:

- Carefully read each question.
- Ponder each question for a while (may be five minutes or five days).
- If you become stuck, seek help from others who know you.
- Write down your answers.
- Carefully review all of your answers and ask yourself, "What does this say about what I should do?"

Question 1—What do I enjoy doing?

Your answers don't necessarily have to be work-related. They can encompass any activity you enjoy both personally and professionally. For some, this is a tough question. Many have spent so much time doing things they *have to do* that they haven't allowed adequate time to think about or do the things they *want to do*. If you are struggling with this question, take a day or two to examine it, yourself, and your past actions and activities before attempting to respond.

Question 2—What do I *not* enjoy doing?

Like the previous question, your answers don't have to be work-related. They can encompass any activity you dislike both personally and professionally. Often, we can uncover what we enjoy doing by listing the things we know we don't enjoy doing—it's a process of elimination. Start by thinking of things you've tried in the past and know you don't enjoy.

Question 3—What do I think I'm good at doing?

Think about those things that come easily or naturally to you—those things others may struggle with, but you do well with ease. Most likely, these are also activities you enjoy and may even do in a volunteer capacity.

Question 4—What do *others* say I'm good at doing?

Some people's talents are obvious like painting, drawing, singing, and dancing. Your gifts may or may not be that easy to recognize. Since gifts and talents are given to us to help others, they may be easier for others to see than you. Don't you always recognize when someone is good at doing something and you aren't? Over the years, have you repeatedly had family members, friends, or colleagues say you do something well? Maybe it's something less obvious like organizing messy spaces or information, working with your hands, analyzing large amounts of data and breaking it into smaller pieces for others to better understand, or generating creative ideas and solutions. Can you recall anyone asking you the following question, "How do you do that so easily?" If you can think of something, more than likely you have talent in that area.

Question 5—What brings you tremendous excitement?

The things that bring you excitement likely are things you enjoy, so why not identify what those are to help ensure you can incorporate them into your work? When you're excited, you're going to be more energized, creative, and engaging—all are attractive traits in the workplace.

Question 6—When was the last time you exceeded expectations? What was it and what caused you to excel?

Were you using a talent that's less obvious? Was it at work, while volunteering, or in your personal life? Were others pleasantly surprised by how well you did or how much you achieved? Do you have a history of exceeding expectations in this manner?

Question 7—Describe the last time you were in "your groove." What were you doing?

One of the ways I know professional speaking is something I'm supposed to do is I feel like I'm in my groove when I'm doing it. I feel like I've just stepped into my true skin. While slight butterflies are initially there, I feel more empowered, more comfortable, and more of myself than I do at most other times. Can you think of things you do that make you feel like this?

Question 8—What topics do you find yourself debating or defending with others? Does your stance represent certain beliefs and interests for you?

People who are passionate about specific subjects find it almost impossible to pass up a good discussion about them. Whether it's challenging someone else's beliefs, sharing information, or offering support, when a topic is near and dear to your heart, usually there's a reason why.

Question 9—How do you most commonly help others, and what do you love helping with the most?

Before I decided to start my speaking and career coaching business, I found myself spending a lot of evenings and weekends helping others with career management and career development issues. This demand helped propel me into my business. How are you spending your time?

Question 10—When was the last time you couldn't sleep because you were so excited about what you were working on?

Well, it may not have kept you awake, but it was certainly work you enjoyed and looked forward to doing more of. It could be a one-time project, working with a particular group of colleagues, or a primary part of your regular work. Regardless, if you could incorporate this into your work going forward, it would increase your fulfillment at work.

Question 11—Of all the work duties in your most recent or current assignment, is there anything you would do for free?

Okay, okay, you may not be willing to do it for your employer for free, but certainly it's something you enjoy a lot. If it went away, you would be disappointed and it would make your days longer. Whether it's a small or significant portion of your work doesn't matter, it makes your work experience much better.

Question 12—If you could write a bestselling book that would help others, what would you write about?

I've read several articles which state as many as ninety percent of American adults say they want to write and publish a book. Whether fiction or nonfiction, people often write about things with which they're familiar—John Grisham was an attorney before he began writing fiction books about the law; Gillian Flynn, who wrote the book turned movie *Gone Girl*, is from Kansas City, Missouri and used Missouri as the setting for her book; I'm writing this book to guide professionals along their career journey to finding more fulfillment and success because this is what I enjoy. Is there something familiar to you or burning inside of you that you'd love to put on paper?

Question 13—What careers have you ever day-dreamed about? What was it about them you liked?

I recommend you think back as far as your early teen years. For most, this was before the pressures to declare a college major, graduate with a degree, find a job, and support a family. Have you thought about any of these careers over the years? Do any of the occupations still excite you? Are any of them reasonably within your grasp now with a little training or extra effort? (Note—if you wanted to play professional sports and are now of a more seasoned age, it's probably not a realistic option!)

Question 14—Think about your core or foundational beliefs or values. What 2-3 careers do you think embody them?

If you're struggling to think of the top two or three, I've included a list of values you can review to help you in the back of this book. Consider those things which are the most important for you in your work. Once you identify your top selections, think of career possibilities that are consistent with your beliefs and values. If you get stuck, solicit help from others to help you brainstorm. You can also conduct an internet search using the words, "Careers that offer [your belief or value]."

Question 15—If you could be a revolutionary for change, what cause would you champion?

One definition of revolution is, "A sudden, complete, or marked changed in something." Another definition refers to radical and pervasive change...accompanied by violence. When you think about being a revolutionary, consider something you're so passionate about, it makes you want to give everything you have to it or make a major sacrifice to get it.

Question 16—What's your favorite section in a library or bookstore and why?

Unless you visit a library or bookstore with limited time to fill a specific need, you'll probably take a few minutes to just browse around and see what's new. Which sections would you visit? What book titles likely would capture your attention first?

Question 17—What are you doing when you are your most confident?

When we do something we enjoy, it's often because we're good at it. When we're good at doing something, it often builds confidence. Think about situations and activities you were engaged in when you felt like you were on top of the world—unstoppable. Review your list from the questions on the previous pages that focused on the areas where you are your best.

Question 18—What would you do if you knew you couldn't fail?

Do you remember the story about King Midas, the mythological king who had the ability to turn everything he touched into gold? This became known as the Midas touch. Imagine you have a similar ability, and everything you do is successful. No matter how difficult, expensive, or outlandish, you were one hundred percent certain to not fail. What would you do?

Question 19—If money weren't an issue, how would you spend your work days?

Imagine this: two years ago you won $350 million dollars in the lottery. You paid off all your bills, bought all of the goodies your heart desires, gave lots of money away, traveled around the world, and now you're back home, with another twenty or more work years ahead of you. You want to make your mark on the world doing something you enjoy, and you now have all of the time and money you need to make it happen. How will you fill your days?

Now, review all of your answers and circle any recurring words or themes you see. On a separate sheet of paper, write all of these words down and study them for a few minutes. What do you see? What do you think? How are you feeling? Are you surprised by anything you see, or are these merely confirmations of things you've already known or suspected? Did you find your bullseye?

If you'll recall, in Chapter Four I discussed how I became bored, burned out, and frustrated with my business and the work I was doing. To help me determine what I wanted to do, I worked through this same exercise. The words that kept showing up for me were speaking, training, career management, and career development. This is how I knew my work in this space wasn't done—it was too engrained in who I was and what I enjoyed. This was also a major catalyst for me to begin writing this book!

Based on your recurring themes, brainstorm a list of at least five careers that make up or include one of your themes. If you can't generate enough ideas on your own, solicit help from family, friends, and professional colleagues, and use the internet as a source.

As a final exercise, over the next month, pay attention to the personal and professional things you enjoy, that attract your attention, or cause you to be more energized and focused. Also, note if someone comments on a particular strength you possess, or if you observe yourself engaged in an activity which is easy for you, but others find difficult. Write what you discover and review it for additional insights.

No matter what you discover, remember this is your journey. Your bullseye may not look like others and that's okay. You may find the work you're doing currently is your bullseye—this is ideal! The goal is not to quit your job and leave your employer, the goal is to find a career path that will bring you fulfillment and success. If you've found it where you are, don't make a move. Enjoy what you're doing and help others to find the same.

Questions to Ponder

1. What are your recurring themes?
2. Are you surprised or did they confirm what you already know? Why?
3. How close or far away from your themes is your most recent or current career path?
4. If you plan to pursue what you've discovered, can this work be done full-time? If not, how about part-time or on a volunteer basis?
5. Are there any barriers you will need to overcome in order to pursue work in alignment your theme area(s)?
6. Do you know others who have found their bullseye? If so, how did they find it, and how is it showing up for them today? Is there anything you can incorporate into your own process of discovery?

CHAPTER 7

Conquering F.E.A.R. with F.E.A.R.

"Everything you've ever wanted is on the other side of fear."
– George Adda

In all of my years of being a career coach, interviewing job seekers, and interacting with audience members after speaking engagements, I've encountered many people who claim to not know what they want to do in their career. When I've probed deeper to understand why not, I've learned that often the root isn't lack of clarity, it's fear. For many, what they want seems so unattainable to them, they won't allow themselves to really want it or even consider the possibility. Over time, they forget about what they used to want or convince themselves they no longer want it. Periodically, it may rear its head, but these same people have become masters of suppression. Can you relate?

While this may go on for a long time, there often comes a day when the frustration of not being true to what you want begins to rear its head. The day-to-day grind becomes less palatable, your patience starts to wear thin, and suddenly the good paycheck is no longer enough. Yet, the mere thought of pursuing what you really want seems overwhelming. The dreaded "what ifs" begin to set in:

- What if I try it and it doesn't work out?
- What if people know I tried it and it doesn't work out?

- What if no one will give me a chance?
- What if I can't do it anymore?
- What if it's too late for me to try it?
- What if I can't afford to try it?
- What if I don't like it?
- What if I can't keep up?
- What if I try and it works, but then I can't sustain it?
- What if...?

Let me just say, the what ifs are some of the more formidable opponents you'll ever face when trying to do anything. They can grab hold of you so tightly that you struggle to breathe, begin to shake, cry, and completely shut down. The what ifs can be so powerful, they can talk you out of something that is a perfect fit. You feel like you have no control over when they'll show up, how long they'll stay, what damage they'll do, and when they'll leave. They are the ultimate bully and the nervous system for fear; they control the flow of life and energy that fear possesses.

Ironically, this very morning when I woke up to begin writing this chapter, I was overcome with fear. It's a Monday, which is always a tough day for me emotionally. I had a really good weekend, and with absolutely no reason to be fearful. Yet, anxiety began to grip me, and the what ifs showed up. "What if I can't figure out what to write?" and "What if I write this book and everyone thinks it's horrible?" and "What if I get sick and die this week?" Yes, the last one just came out of nowhere, yet it came and occupied my mind for several minutes. Like other bullies, the what ifs also don't fight fairly!

Even in the midst of my own what ifs battle, I still had to do what I'm going to share with you in the following paragraphs and pages. It's the best way I've found to push through the fears in my life to keep pressing forward, and I believe they will help you, too.

In order to overcome fear, you must first understand it better. There are three types of fear that people experience:

1. Fear of change
2. Fear of failure
3. Fear of success

Fear of Change

Psychologists diagnose people with severe fear of change with metathesiophobia. It has been linked to tropophobia, fear of moving. As humans, most of us are wired to be creatures of habit—to remain in a known, comfortable state or place. We take the same route to and from work, shop at the same grocery stores, buy the same brand of toothpaste, and sleep on the same side of the bed. We may not mind small changes in our work or life routines, but major changes can shake us off our foundation. In work situations, many convince themselves that change is bad, and even deny change is coming.

I once worked for a company with many diverse business divisions. Over the years, the company began to spin off the different divisions, and rumors spread that the company was preparing for a buyout. When the announcement finally came of the acquisition, I was shocked by the people who were shocked! I couldn't believe it when I heard two director-level employees, who had greater access to this type of business activity than most, telling several employees there wouldn't be many changes. They said the new organization would primarily have a presence in name only. Boy were their heads buried deep in the sand! There ended up being several rounds of layoffs, leadership was brought in from the new parent company, and things have never been the same.

When people are faced with major change, it forces them to confront some of the very what ifs listed previously like "What if I don't like it?" and "What if I can't keep up?" Fear of change is so pervasive that a thirty-two-page non-fiction book on dealing with change became a bestseller in 1998. *Who Moved My Cheese*, by Spencer Johnson, remained on the *New York Times* business bestseller list for almost five years. It spent over 200 weeks on *Publishers Weekly's* hardcover nonfiction list, has sold over 28 million copies worldwide, and has been published in thirty-seven languages.

I remembered hearing so much about this book when it was introduced that, immediately, I went out and purchased it (I needed help dealing with change too!). The book made some good points, but I was amazed at how such a small, and what appeared to be simple, book could grab hold of the masses. People around the world were struggling with change and seeking answers.

Fear of Failure

Fear of failure is probably the most popular of the three fears. While no one *likes* to fail, some manage to make the most of failure, putting it in perspective and persevering in their quest for success. Take Thomas Edison. He failed over and over while attempting new inventions including the light bulb and a new type of storage battery. The authorized biography of Thomas Edison, *Edison: His Life and Inventions* by Frank Dyer and T.C. Martin quote Edison's friend, Walter S. Mallory, regarding one conversation he had with Edison about his many experiments. He asked, "Isn't it a shame that with the tremendous amount of work you have done you haven't been able to get any results?" Edison responded, "Results! Why, man, I have gotten lots of results! I know several thousand things that won't work!"

Michael Jordan, one of the greatest basketball players of all time, once shot a Nike commercial where he almost lauded his failures. He stated, "I've missed more than nine thousand shots in my career. I've lost almost 300 games. Twenty-six times I've been trusted to take the game-winning shot and missed. I've failed over, and over, and over again in my life, and that is why I succeed."

While some view failure as another opportunity to get it right, others see it as a doomsday scenario. When your perspective about failure causes you to stop doing things that can move you forward to achieve your goals, this is called atychiphobia. People with this disorder may try to justify why they can't or won't do something because of a past experience, or because there isn't enough time, or they don't have enough money. These reasons are used to convince themselves and others that the pursuit wouldn't be good for them. It's a great way to remain safe in a cocoon, but it doesn't free a person from the circumstances from which they want relief.

The what ifs appear quite frequently and aggressively when there is a fear of failure. The what-if bully sees this as a prime time to attack, and throws out the scariest, most stressful what ifs possible—"What if I try it and it doesn't work out?" and "What if people know I tried it and it doesn't work out?" There's a feeling of being a loser and being embarrassed at the same time. As humans, we loathe feeling embarrassed or humiliated. If we try something that isn't successful, we now must face the people we told we could do it that we failed. Not fun! The irony is most people are genuinely disappointed for the other person when they hear about them failing, especially those they know personally. There's a part of us that tends to internalize it as a possibility that the same thing could happen to us, and it causes us to have more empathy for others when they fail. Have you ever watched a game show with the same intensity as the actual players, and then winced or screamed out loud when they lost? Or, ever wonder why the good guy or gal usually wins at the end of a movie? It's because we like to see people win. It makes us feel good and helps us believe we can be winners, too.

Fear of Success

This type of fear frequently goes unrecognized. We are so accustomed to considering failure as our fate that we often don't realize that the opposite could be the culprit—success. Actually, I think I've suffered more from this type of fear than the fear of change or failure. I began recognizing it in myself over ten years ago. When I would consider doing something new or different, my knee-jerk thoughts weren't about the magnitude of the change or the embarrassment of a possible failure. My biggest concerns centered around if it worked, could I handle everything that came along with success in that area?

You may think being fearful of success is arrogant, but let me share why it's not. When this occurs, there's a tug-of-war taking place between confidence and humility. On one hand, you believe you have certain abilities or resources to achieve your goal. On the other hand, you're fearful of adequately being able to manage the success that can come from your efforts. You know there's always the possibility of failure, but you're more optimistic that your efforts will bring you closer to immediate success.

This is another time when the what ifs will knock. "What if I get promoted and I can't handle the new job?" or "What if I'm put in charge of the project and project team, and I don't know how to lead either?" You see, the fear is not about hitting one milestone; it's about hitting the larger milestones that may come afterwards! The fear of success is merely an off-shoot of the fear of failure— only delayed.

F.E.A.R. versus F.E.A.R.

When it comes to addressing your fears, you can overcome them by understanding F.E.A.R., and how to use it to win. I learned a definition of fear years ago. The pastor at my church was addressing the concerns many people have when stepping out to act on faith. He told us we must remember what fear really was—**False Evidence Appearing Real**. This was, and still is, the best definition I've ever heard for it.

At the end of the day, every what if you imagine is nothing more than false evidence appearing real. The key word is *appearing*; it hasn't actually happened. You stress yourself out over something you've conjured up in your mind. There's no physical evidence of its manifestation. If you look back over your career and life, likely you'll discover over ninety-five percent of the time, the what ifs you worry about never occur. You may even forget you had them.

When you set a goal and begin to feel fear as a result, remind yourself that the thoughts are only in your mind; *nothing has actually happened.* You're in the same position as you were immediately before you had the thoughts. As you begin to remind yourself of this truth and meditate on it, this can cause your emotions to calm down, so you can begin to think and act more rationally about your goal and how to achieve it. I have used this technique over the years and it's proven to be quite effective.

If you find yourself struggling to overcome the notion that the what ifs are only in your mind, use another F.E.A.R. to address it—**Face Everything and Respond**. Write down every what if scenario you can imagine as it relates to your circumstance or achieving your goal. One-by-one, think through the worst-case scenario and write down a short plan for how you can address it. If or when you encounter the circumstance, pull out your plan and then address it!

There are times in life when you can't shy away from a struggle. You must look it in the eye and deal with it. This is how I felt when it came to writing this book; my first book that I was determined to complete. I had dreamed of doing this for years, but always came up with a reason why it wasn't the right time, or I didn't have time, or I wasn't sure of what to write. Finally, a day came when I realized I would have to overcome F.E.A.R. (False Evidence Appearing Real) and demonstrate F.E.A.R. (Face Everything and Respond) in order to get it done. I literally looked at myself in my bathroom mirror and said, "This time, no excuses. You WILL write this book NOW!" To help me not backdown, I contacted a professional author consultant I knew, told her I was ready, and paid the necessary money to get the process started. I put my money where my goal was. The rest is what you're now reading.

While the majority of this chapter has focused on addressing the negative side of fear, there is also a positive side. When you set a goal and begin to feel fear as you contemplate it or start to act, it can mean you're stretching yourself beyond your current state, which is a good thing. The only way to grow is by being enlarged, or stretched. Ellen Johnson Sirleaf, the first woman President of an African nation, is quoted in her memoir, *"This Child Will Be Great: Memoir of a Remarkable Life,"* as saying, "If your dreams do not scare you, they are not big enough." If your goal can be easily attained, what's the point in making it a goal? Just add it to your to-do list for tomorrow and get it done.

There are also positive what ifs you can consider:
- What if I try and achieve my goal?
- What if I try and exceed my goal?
- What if I'm really good at what I do?
- What if I end up more fulfilled than I have ever been?
- What if other people are excited for me and celebrate my success with me?
- What if my success leads to other opportunities which are even better?
- What if my timing is perfect?
- What if…?

Remember, most of the fears you encounter are often made up of a series of what ifs that are like the wizard in *The Wizard of Oz*. They blow a lot of smoke and make a lot of noise, but as soon as you pull back the drape, really there's not much there.

Questions to Ponder

1. Can you think of a goal your fears have stopped you from pursuing or achieving? If so, discuss what the goal was and what stopped you.
2. Have you ever discovered a fear you had wasn't even real?

3. If you set a goal in the past for which fear kept you from achieving, what can you do now to press past the fear and move forward with your goal?

4. Do the acronyms F.E.A.R. (False Evidence Appearing Real) and F.E.A.R. (Face Everything and Respond) resonate with you? If so, how and why?

5. Are you currently working on a goal which stretches you beyond your comfort level? How can you be proactive in keeping the what ifs and F.E.A.R. (False Evidence Appearing Real) away?

6. What must you F.E.A.R. (Face Everything and Respond) in order to achieve your goal?

CHAPTER 8

Demonstrate What You Want Before You Get It

"How can you expect your ship to come in if you don't send one out?"
– Author Unknown

In any career, one of the most burdensome feelings you can have is not knowing what you want to do. It can create a mental paralysis that causes you to remain in terrible conditions much longer than you should. Lack of clarity can abuse your confidence, erode your self-esteem, and cause fear and panic to set in. Your decisions become harder to make and the thought of making a change becomes too overwhelming to consider.

We live in a world that rewards and expects action and achievement. When you aren't in action mode, and therefore not achieving what you think you should be (or what you think others expect of you), you start to doubt yourself. You question your ability to accomplish, and begin to ask yourself questions like, "What's wrong with me?" and "Why can't I get out of this rut?" If you've ever been in this place and then gained clarity, you know the exhilaration you feel by simply figuring out what you want. You may not have taken one step toward making it happen, but the burden of not knowing is gone. That's often enough to revive many of the places within us we thought had dried up—our confidence, energy, creativity, and assertiveness.

So, when you know what you want and there's little or no fear of going after it, what's next? The answer is it depends upon whether what you want to pursue is a hop, skip, and a jump away, or a quantum leap. If your goal is familiar to you and you already know what it will take to achieve it, then research what's required and begin working on it. For example, you know you want to be promoted to a project manager role and have great experience, but you know you need a Project Management Professional certification in order to make it happen. Find out how to get certified and do it!

If your goal requires more of a quantum leap—for example, you work in Engineering but want to work in Finance—this may take more time and effort to achieve. It may require you to conduct research, do extra work on the job, return to school, volunteer, network, find a mentor and sponsor, take a pay cut, and pray! It may also require you to demonstrate what you want before you get it.

Demonstrate What You Want Before You Get It—An Analogy

Let me share an analogy to illustrate my point—this is what I call my "duck story," and it's my story about how man first discovered duck for food. Many years ago, a lost and starving man was walking near a lake. He noticed an odd-looking dead animal at his feet—a duck. As he stopped to observe it, the thought of his hunger and potential food came to his mind, and he wondered if the animal could be eaten. Since he was so hungry, he decided to take a chance and eat it. As he began to consume the dead carcass, he decided it was one of the tastiest morsels of food he ever had.

Once he regained his strength, he continued his journey and eventually found his way back to his tribe. With excitement, he told them about the tasty animal he had found. They became so intrigued that they decided to go back to where he first saw the animal to try and hunt them to eat. When they arrived, he pointed out the bird with excitement as he noticed an entire flock of them wading in shallow water. Immediately, the men began yelling and screaming as they ran toward the duck. They were startled and dismayed when the ducks began to swim and fly away. Once they realized their efforts were futile, they sadly bowed their heads and walked away still hungry.

For several days, they repeated this ritual, but failed to capture any ducks. After their fourth day of attempts, the elder hunter (who was retired and now a supervisor, but still liked to join the hunts) shared a keen observation. "You know, I've been watching these birds and watching your attempts to hunt them, and I think you're doing it all wrong. I've noticed when the birds move slowly and make this funny sound toward one another (quack, quack), they move closer together, but when you run after them yelling and screaming, they run and fly off. You might want to slow down and try making that funny noise to see what happens."

The hunters initially laughed at this recommendation, but later decided they should at least give it a try. The next day, several of the men observed the ducks for a few minutes, attempted to make the noise, and moved at a slower pace toward them. While the ducks still swam and flew away, there was a hesitancy in their efforts. The hunters noticed this and became very encouraged. For one week, they stayed home to perfect their noise so they sounded more like the ducks.

When they felt confident with their imitation of a duck, they went hunting again. This time, when they moved slowly in the ducks' direction and made their more perfected sound, the ducks began to swim toward them. One duck even moved so close that a hunter was able to capture it. The other birds noticed this and flew away, but the hunters were thrilled at their success. They continued to work at perfecting their sound and, over time, created an actual tool to be used specifically for duck hunting—the duck call—which is used by thousands of hunters today.

Before I go on, let me just say I have no idea if this is the process by which man discovered duck as food, but I bet there are some similarities! It had to begin somewhere, right? What I'm trying to demonstrate through this analogy is before the men could achieve their goal (capturing a duck), they had to first demonstrate what was required in order to get it (duck sounds). Once they demonstrated it effectively, they got the duck and enjoyed a tasty meal.

This same approach may be required for you to achieve your career goal. Rarely will you be able to achieve what you want by yourself—you'll need help from someone. Depending on who you need, most likely you'll have to demonstrate a level of readiness before you ever get it.

Demonstrating what you want before you get it is my code phrase for saying you must "show up." I don't mean you must physically be present, although this is important! I mean you must demonstrate the **performance and behaviors** required for others to believe you're ready for more or different. Further, these must be demonstrated *before* you receive the prize.

In today's society, employers are much more risk averse than in years past, because of the significantly increased number of lawsuits and, of course, social media. As a result, they may be more hesitant to place an inexperienced person in an advanced position. Thus, if you haven't demonstrated an adequate degree of readiness before being placed in an assignment, there's a good chance it won't happen.

Anyone who's managed or led people understands it takes a different skill set to do a job versus *leading people* who do a job. Many individual contributors don't understand this and become frustrated when they want to get promoted to a supervisory-level position, but aren't being moved up or seriously considered. My question to those individual contributors—have you been *demonstrating* leadership, or have you been demonstrating all of the traits required to be a great individual contributor? Have you been "showing up" as a leader? There is a difference.

Individual contributors who aspire for more are quick to point out the following four things when they're trying to convince others they're ready for more responsibility:

I. **They are hard workers.** They arrive early, stay late, and produce more completed work than anyone else on the team. Their performance reviews always reflect how hard they work and how much work they complete. They receive compliments all the time regarding how hard they work.

II. **They don't cause problems.** They aren't the ones spreading false information on the team or in the department. They haven't had any conflicts with anyone, and usually operate as the peacemaker within the group.

III. **They color within the lines.** Whatever deadline is given to them, they meet. If there is a budget they're required to manage, they always complete the assignment under budget. No matter what the parameters are for their work, they always meet or exceed them. They are very good at operating within the boundaries.

IV. **They have a good attitude.** Even when they don't agree with the team/department/company decision, they always find the silver lining. They can always be found with a smile on their face, and are viewed by others as the "sunshine of the department."

All four of these traits are important to demonstrate at work, and are realistic expectations for an employer to have of an employee. However, are these the critical traits *required for leadership*, or for leadership within your organization? If you're demonstrating these traits and still aren't getting the results you want, there may be more that's required. You may be walking at a slower pace to catch your duck, but still aren't making the right sound.

The key is you must do your homework to find out what's required—it may not be what you think. You must invest the time and effort to better understand. You can do this by reading a job description for the desired position, observing those in the position you want, discussing the requirements with your boss, or seeking counsel from a mentor or sponsor.

In the over twenty-five years I worked in corporate professional assignments, I learned there are some unwritten requirements at every level that can play a role in your career advancement. These requirements won't be seen in any job description, but they are important nevertheless. The following illustration shows a generic organization structure (because every structure is differ-ent) which outlines some of those unwritten requirements that often help demonstrate to others a person's readiness for career advancement:

Unwritten Rules for Career Advancement

Executive/Partner/ Vice President+ — Thinks inwardly, vertically, horizontally and externally (Builds performance + impact + relationships and internal influence + external credibility and capability)

Director — Thinks inwardly, vertically and horizontally (Builds performance + impact + relationships and internal influence)

Manager — Thinks inwardly and vertically (Builds performance + impact)

Individual Contributor — Thinks inwardly (Builds performance)

©2018 Bernie Frazier. All Rights Reserved

As an **individual contributor**, your primary focus is **inward**. You focus on your performance, how you show up, your deadlines, your performance reviews, your salary increases, etc. The only oth-er person you have to focus on is your supervisor. At this level, your goal is to build your **performance**. You must ensure you're meeting the expectations and requirements of the job in order to maintain your employment. Yet, when you aspire to become a manager, to lead other people, the requirements expand.

As a **manager**, your focus remains inward, because you must still successfully perform the duties of your job. However, you must also focus **vertically** which includes your supervisor, your perfor-mance, and the performance of those with whom you lead—you must **consider what is happening above** *and below* **you**. Your work must have impact in your department or organization, and this must be accomplished through others—the same others who require you to motivate, calm down, praise, correct, and just plain figure them out—all at the same time. You must lead a "motley crew" in a way that causes them to perform and deliver at a high level for the organization and for you. Your goals are to build **performance and have impact**. After a few years of successfully performing at the manager-level, you may decide you want to be a director.

As a **director**, you must still satisfy the requirements of the individual contributor and manager, but now must add a level of focus which is **horizontal**. In many instances, once you reach the director level, you're not actually involved in the day-to-day work; you're leading those who are leading others in doing the work. As a director, it becomes more important for you to **build internal relationships with your peers and superiors**. You are more likely to be involved in or leading cross-functional or cross-divisional teams. Your work becomes more strategic and you may be leading multiple teams or even departments, therefore impacting more of your organization's bottom line. When you reach this level, it becomes more important for others to know *you* and not just your work. They need to feel comfortable in knowing you can handle and drive major parts of the business. At this level, you must continue to monitor your individual performance and still have impact, but now must build **solid relationships** in order to win the support of others and drive the business forward.

The last and final level is the **executive (or partner/vice president and above)** level. While still satisfying the requirements of the other three levels, the final piece of the puzzle for this level is being able to think and operate **externally**. At the executive level, you may need to break new ground or move the organization into unchartered waters which often requires **connections and good will outside of the organization**. Ever notice when there's new information to be announced by an organization, if a public relations/community affairs employee isn't serving as the organization's spokesperson, an executive does it? I once worked for an organization that was looking to build a new facility in a different municipality. The executive who was sharing about the progress mentioned a lunch meeting he had with one of the aldermen in that municipality. Of course, the goal was to help strengthen ties with that community to gain a "yes" vote for the new facility. He was working to **build the organization's credibility in order to build its capability**.

Did you know about these other expectations at the different levels before reading this? Are you aware of what the unwritten expectations are in your organization? If not, you may be the best worker at your level, but still never achieve the success you desire because you aren't currently demonstrating what's required at the level you now want to operate, and convincing them *right now* that you're ready for more.

I realize not everyone wants to be promoted up in their career and there's absolutely nothing wrong with this. Some people want to make a lateral move, or leave their current employer for different pastures. However, the principle is the same—you must demonstrate what you want before you get it. If you want to transfer into a different department to do a different type of job, the decision-makers still want to make sure they make a good selection when hiring. If you've been demonstrating what's required through your performance and behaviors, your chances of success often increase significantly. They know what they want and have already seen it in you—that's a great set up for "You're hired!"

As a veteran talent acquisition professional and leader, I can tell you that prospective employers definitely look for past demonstrations of what's required. A new employer doesn't know you, your work, personality, or potential like your current or most recent employer. Therefore, their level of scrutiny will be higher, so being able to demonstrate the requirements on paper, online, in-person, and through those in your network, is critical for achieving your goal.

By now you should understand whether you're seeking a promotion, lateral move within or outside your current work area, or new position with another employer, often there are unwritten requirements that can take more effort to find and understand than what you see on the surface. It's critical that you understand what others need to see in order to help you achieve your career goals. You may or may not agree with what they need to see, but if they hold the key to your next step, you must find a way to come to terms with their requirements.

What is or isn't seen?

While working in Human Resources, I had an opportunity to observe and participate in succession planning sessions. If you aren't familiar with this concept, succession planning is a process used by many organizations to identify and develop potential future leaders or senior managers, as well as individuals, to fill other positions critical to an organization. This can be either in the short or the long term. It usually involves pre-work by the leaders, and then a gathering of these leaders to discuss current employees, their potential, and next steps. In one of my corporate Human Resources assignments, I played a dual role in this process—I was an observer/participant as well as a subject for discussion, because it was my level in the organization being discussed—thanks DC!

I had not participated in succession planning meetings before and was quite curious to see how they work. As a manager, I was one of the three lowest ranking members in the meeting—everyone else was either a director, vice president, or the president of the organization. I must admit it was a bit intimidating. A grid, called a Nine Box, was used to slot each manager based on their past demonstrations of performance and behavior. The manager's supervisor would confirm their employee's placement on the grid, and then provide their justification for the placement. Once done, other leaders would comment with their thoughts of agreement or disagreement.

		Low	Moderate	High
Potential Assessment	High	Low Performer/ High Potential	Moderate Performer/High Potential	High Performer/ High Potential
	Moderate	Low Performer/ Moderate Potential	Moderate Performer/ Moderate Potential	High Performer/ Moderate Potential
	Low	Low Performer/ Low Potential	Moderate Performer/Low Potential	High Performer/ Low Potential

Performance Assessment

As the hours rolled by, I began to notice something very interesting. Once a supervisor completed their placement announcement and justification and others began to chime in with their opinions, I started hearing two phrases:

"I can see..."

"I can't see..."

The leaders would intently listen and then state things like, "I have to be honest. *I can't see* him in that role. In my experiences..." or "I think you're spot on. *I can definitely see* that she's ready for more because..." I heard these phrases over and over again. Isn't it ironic that these leaders were basing their opinions and stated positions on what they could and couldn't *see*? What they were saying was, from their perspective, the person being evaluated had or hadn't *already* demonstrated the performance and behaviors needed for the next opportunity based on the requirements for that opportunity. They had or hadn't previously demonstrated the characteristics for success.

Isn't that interesting? Most of them didn't display documented data and statistics to support their claims. They were merely basing their evaluations on their knowledge of what's really required and their past experiences and exposures to the managers being discussed. This is precisely why having a track record of demonstrated performance and behaviors is so important. Even if you are the most qualified (on paper), hardest working person being considered for an opportunity, you may not be considered seriously if others haven't seen your potential already.

Questions to Ponder

1. Have you had an experience where someone you knew was pursuing a goal, but you could see they weren't ready for it? Were they aware of the "unwritten rules" for achieving their goal?

2. Looking back, can you think of a time when you pursued a goal, but weren't fully aware of what was required to achieve it, therefore you missed the mark? What did you learn from this? How did you course correct?

3. Currently, who or what is your duck? What are you doing to ensure you're an effective hunter?

4. What are the performance and behavior requirements for your goal? Are you currently demonstrating them?

5. Would it be easy for others to see your demonstrations of expected performance and behaviors for what you want to achieve?

Chapter 9

Create and Execute Against a Plan

"Planning is bringing the future into the present so that you can do something about it now."
– Alan Lakein

If you've ever felt stuck in your career, you know the terrific feeling of finally having a breakthrough, a goal. The skies are bluer, the air smells cleaner, and food tastes better. The helplessness you felt turns into empowerment, and you're ready to conquer the world! You may even share this with others who are excited for you and support you in your efforts. It's a great day!

As wonderful as it is to have a breakthrough, it's important to remember this is just one step in the process. The next step is doing something about it. You need to create a plan and put it in motion. For some, this is a no-brainer. For others, it's as painful as having a tooth pulled without Novocain. Yet, if you're to ever enjoy achieving your goal, you must create a plan and execute it.

The overwhelming majority of people won't bump into career success like the American actress, Rosario Dawson. She has starred in numerous movies including *Men in Black II, Rent, Justice League: Throne of Atlantis, Justice League vs. Teen Titans, He Got Game*, and many others. She was discovered on her front-porch step by photographer Larry Clark and Harmony Korine. Korine believed she was perfect for a role he had written in his screenplay-turned-film, *Kids*. Since then, Dawson has starred in almost fifty films. She bumped into success, or should I say, success bumped into her!

Dawson's story is a wonderful way to ignite a career, but it's not realistic for most, including most Hollywood megastars. If you were to interview many of them, they would share their tales of working two and three jobs to make ends meet while taking acting lessons, showing up for auditions, networking, exercising, and doing the other activities required to be "discovered." Their success took planning and action.

Why do I have to plan?

Not good at planning and think you can work around it? I want you to do this exercise before deciding against it.

Step 1	Think about the last big vacation you took (by big, I mean at least one week; could be domestic or international), and the month and year in which you began your vacation planning. Now, think about the month and year in which the vacation took place. Write down how much time passed between the planning and the actual vacation dates? Was it weeks or months?
Step 2	Record this statement, "I spent [fill in the time] weeks/months planning for a [fill in the time] week vacation." For instance, I began planning for a one-week vacation in January 2017 which I didn't take until July 2017. This means I spent six months planning for a one-week vacation.

Step 3	Consider how much time (in years) has passed since you began your career. Add up and record the amount of time you've spent planning for your career to-date?
Step 4	Record this statement, "I've spent [fill in the time] weeks/months/years planning for all [fill in the time] years of my career."
Step 5	Consider how many years you have left in your career, then record how much time you've spent planning for the future of your career.
Step 6	Record this statement, "I've spent [fill in the time] weeks/months/years planning for all [fill in the time] years left in my career."
Step 7	Review your recorded statements, and compare the amount of time you spent planning for your vacation to the amount of time you've spent planning for your career, past and future.

Shocking, isn't it? Every time I introduce this exercise to clients and audiences, participants are stunned by their results. Are you? Most people fail to consider they will spend thirty-five to forty-five years, on average, in their career, but spend very little time planning for it. Yet, they will spend months planning for a vacation that will only last one-to-two weeks! It's no wonder almost seventy percent of U.S. and eighty-seven percent of global employees are disengaged at work. They haven't *planned* for anything better!

In 1979, Harvard University conducted a study with their MBA program students. They asked the students, "Have you set clear, written goals for your future and made plans to accomplish them?" When they received and tallied the results, they discovered eighty-four percent had no specific goals, and thirteen percent had goals but hadn't written them down. Only three percent had clearly written goals and plans.

Ten years later, Harvard interviewed these same students to find out where they were in their careers. What they discovered was simply amazing. The thirteen percent which previously had goals, but nothing written down, were earning, on average, twice as much as the eighty-four percent who had no goals. What was even more amazing is the three percent who had clearly written goals and plans were earning ten times as much as the other ninety-seven percent combined! The primary difference was planning.

When it was time to execute against a plan, only the three percent had a plan to reference. The eighty-four percent were clueless and probably ended up going down a path they later regretted. The thirteen percent probably had a great goal but, later, couldn't remember what it was and moved on to other things.

If you don't create a plan, I have two questions for you:

1. **How do you stay focused?**

    You can have the most brilliant idea that can generate the most amazing results, but if you don't write it down and create a plan for how you will achieve it, it's difficult to remain focused on it. This great idea now has to compete for space in your brain with everything else happening in your life—deciding what you'll eat for dinner, following up on the many emails and phone calls at work, trying to remember the items on the grocery list you left at home, maneuvering through the traffic accident to make it to the gym on time, preparing for your performance review, among the many others.

    These work and life distractions occur every day. This means your brilliant idea may move further and further out of your memory and priorities if you aren't diligent enough to keep it front-and-center, and monitor your progress. Of course, you can't always keep it at the top of your priority list, but when you must temporarily move it down the list to address other matters, having a written plan will help you to remember where you left off and what now needs to be addressed when your focus returns to the plan.

2. Who holds you accountable?

When you're working on a goal, I believe in limiting how much and with whom you share until an appropriate time. As my mother has said all of my life, "Sometimes you just have to do it and then talk about it." Yet, when what you're working on requires tremendous effort and can take time to achieve, I believe you should share it with at least one person who can hold you accountable.

It's easy to begin an endeavor with great excitement and energy, but it can take real grit to see it through until the end. You need someone else to hold you accountable in those moments of weakness. This person will remind you of why you started the endeavor in the first place, and push you to move forward. You need some iron in your life! As a scripture in the Bible states, "As iron sharpens iron, so one person sharpens another." This is true. If you try to sharpen a knife with a cotton ball, the knife will remain dull. Yet, if you sharpen it with another piece of equally strong or stronger material, it can be re-sharpened as if it were brand new. Share your goal with another who is strong enough to hold you accountable and watch how they work. You *will* reach your goal!

Years ago, I started exercising with a good friend. We met two-to-four times a week after work, and would engage in various forms of exercise for at least one hour. While it was always great to see her, I didn't always feel like going to gym after working all day. However, I still made it on those days because I knew she'd be there waiting on me. I was accountable to her and knew she'd have something to say if I stood her up. The funny thing is, when I arrived on those days and shared how I felt, she often felt the same way, but showed up for the same reason. Guess who's my accountability partner for writing this book? You guessed it, that same friend!

Accountability is a powerful tool for achieving goals. Don't go anywhere without it!

Let's Do This Plan!

Creating a plan doesn't have to be a complicated endeavor, and there's more than one way to do it. It can be as simple or complicated as you want—the main thing is to have one! When I need to create a plan, I use a document I created from my years of seeing planning documents in Corporate America. It contains the following sections:

GOAL:					
KEY STRATEGIES	**ACTION STEPS**	**MONITOR**		**MEASURE**	
		Due Date	Notes	Desired Result	Actual Result

Goal: Outlines the main thing you want to accomplish. It could be to get promoted, find a new job within your current employer, transition your career, find a new job elsewhere, or something else. You want to make sure your goal is large enough for which a plan can be created. There is no right or wrong wording for your goal, but you may want to consider using the S.M.A.R.T. Goal™ method developed by George T. Doran. I believe it challenges you to think more comprehensively about your goal.

Strategies: One definition of strategy is a plan of action or policy designed to achieve a major or overall aim. When you think about the strategies, consider those major efforts required to achieve your goal. For example, if your goal were to lose weight, one strategy may be to understand the types of food which are more likely to cause weight gain or loss. In order to make your goal attainable, I recommend generating no more than five strategies.

Action Steps: These are the specific steps you must take in order to achieve the strategy with which they are associated. Your action steps can be as small as making a phone call, but if that call (and what you gain from it) is important to achieving the strategy, adding it to the document makes sense. I recommend no more than seven action steps. This isn't a hard-and-fast rule, but I recommend you avoid generating so many action items that you become overwhelmed.

Due Date: Each action item should have a corresponding due date, which is a major part of your accountability and one of the main things upon which your accountability partner will focus. When selecting dates, carefully consider what's involved in achieving the action steps, including what could go wrong or cause a delay. Your dates should stretch you, but also be attainable. Also, since life happens, realize you may have to adjust dates because you weren't able to achieve the step during the time listed. This is okay and happens—just remember to add a new date and keep moving forward.

Notes: Record any notes about your action items or due dates— unexpected occurrences, major wins, setbacks, follow ups, key names, etc. Record anything that is key to know, remember, or act upon regarding that action item or due date.

Monitor: A reminder to pay attention to your due dates and any follow ups from your notes. Time goes by quickly and if you aren't monitoring your calendar, you could miss important dates or necessary follow ups.

Desired Result: From the action items listed, record the result you're hoping to achieve. This is your ideal state if everything for the action item goes according to plan.

Actual Result: Once the action item is completed, record what result you actually achieved. It may be the same as your desired result, but it's not uncommon to achieve something slightly different.

Measure: Once you have the actual result, compare it to your desired result to determine if your results are close or far apart. If far apart, examine what may have happened to cause the gap. If this is something you'll have to repeat, you can now devise a solution to bring your desired and actual results closer together.

As you complete the documenting of your plan, there are two important points to remember. First, your plan is a living document. Since you can't control all of the circumstances you'll encounter, your plan is only your best guess. Certainly, the unexpected will occur. When it does, re-evaluate your plan and make the necessary adjustments so you can continue moving forward. Second, this type of document can be used to plan life or business goals, so don't hesitate to adapt them for those needs as needed.

Doing the Work

The title of this Chapter is Creating *and Executing Against* a Plan. I'm reminding you of this, because there is a second part to what you must do to achieve your goal and experience success—execute. It's one thing to create a fantastic written plan and identify an accountability partner, it's another to start doing the work. Unfortunately, the planning stage is where many goals stop living. The great motivational speaker, Les Brown, says it this way:

> *"The graveyard is the richest place on earth, because it is here that you will find all the hopes and*
> *dreams that were never fulfilled, the books that were never written, the songs that were never sung,*

the inventions that were never shared, the cures that were
never discovered, all because someone
was too afraid to take that first step, keep with the problem,
or determined to carry out their dream."

Many people have had identified goals for their career and even developed a plan for achieving those goals. Yet, when it's time to act on their plan, they take minimal or no steps toward achievement. In Chapter Four, I said, "…at the end of the day, nothing and no one can cause you to choose the changes you need for a better career—only you can do this. The old saying, "If it's going to be, it's up to me" never rang truer than right here, right now. This is your career—no one else's. No matter how much people love and care about you, no matter how invested others are in your success, until YOU choose to make a change, nothing will change—at least, none of the changes made will stick." It remains true in this chapter too.

There always will be obstacles to overcome to achieve your goal, but you'll never reach it if you don't push toward it. The world isn't designed to give you your heart's desire without your effort. You'll have to push "go" and then get going. I've wanted to write (and complete) a book for years, but until I began writing it, it wasn't going to happen. I want you to succeed and I'm sure many others want the same for you, but none of us are equipped to do it for you. You can do it, just start… today!

Questions to Ponder

1. Describe a pursuit you have planned for. Was it written? Did you execute against it? What were your results?

2. Do you have a plan for your career goal(s)? If yes, describe it. Is it written down? Does anyone else know about it?

3. How did planning for your last vacation compare to planning for your career—past or future? Are you surprised? Can you identify any changes needed to plan for the future of your career?

4. When pursuing a goal, what helps you remain focused through completion? What are your biggest distractions/ excuses?

5. Who or what holds you accountable when pursuing a goal? How is this done?

6. What excuses have you used in the past to delay the pursuit of a goal, if any? Were they legitimate? What was the result?

CHAPTER 10

Staying the Course

"Today's mighty oak is just yesterday's nut who held its ground."
– David Icke

S uccess is never easy to attain. If it were, everyone would be successful! For some, the most difficult part of achieving success is figuring out in what area they want it. For others, the challenge is sustaining the momentum while pursuing it, because it can take time, a lot of effort, and the will to overcome obstacles. While there is no silver bullet for staying on course, I want to share four things you can do to help push through the tough times, so you can achieve your goal.

Expect Tough Times

You *will* experience tough times. I have absolutely no scientific data to support this, but I have *never* known or heard of anyone who has achieved success without experiencing some tough times. Have you? If you know of anyone who has, please tell them to write the book! I'll be the first person to buy a copy. In Chapter Nine, I mentioned how quickly and easily Rosario Dawson began her acting career. It may have begun easily, but I bet a private conversation with her would garner you some interesting stories of the challenges she's faced since being discovered.

When you start your journey, you may not be able to anticipate what kind of hardships you'll face. Just know they will come. This knowledge will help you be prepared to address challenges, and be able to rebound faster.

Like millions, correction billions, of people around the globe, I enjoy perusing and interacting with people I know on Facebook. A couple of years ago, a friend posted the following picture. Seeing it literally caused me to stop what I was doing!

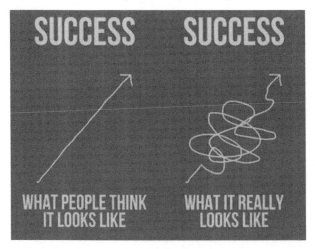

Success is messy, and hard, and frustrating, and scary, and confusing, and painful, and…. However, when you achieve it, it's one of the sweetest things you'll ever experience. Over the decades, I've heard plenty of horror stories about pregnancy and childbirth. What happens to a woman physically, mentally, and emotionally are unimaginable for someone like me who doesn't have children.

Yet, every mother will tell you gladly they'd do it again to get to the sweet reward that awaited them.

Keep Your Goal in Front of You

The week before I wrote this chapter, a friend shared a powerful story with me about focus. I knew part of it, but she filled in the blanks and, when she was done, I knew I had to include it in this book. The story is about her son, who I've known all his life. What she shared about this teenager's journey to achieving a big goal he wanted is simply fantastic.

Daniel (not his real name) is a bright, talented athlete. Over the years, he played several sports, but began to settle into basketball during his middle school years. During this same period, he decided he wanted to play Division I basketball for a large, state school. If you know anything about college sports, you know this isn't an easy feat. There are thousands of talented kids all over the country vying for these coveted spots each year.

Over the next few years, she would ask him which school he wanted to attend—he couldn't answer. Finally, he figured it out and shared his target school with her. He continued to play throughout high school and, often, would awaken very early in the morning to exercise and practice so he could continue to improve his performance. He was a star player, so everything looked good for his future.

However, during Daniel's senior year in high school, things began to unravel. He started encountering unwarranted, major opposition from some of the very people he needed (or thought he needed) to achieve his goal. To the average adult, the circumstances would have brought frustration and a bit of fear, but Daniel was a teenager, and the challenge shook him to his core. His goal seemed to be slipping away from him. All his hard work was going down the drain.

For the next year, Daniel had to shift his efforts in another direction. Yet, he continued to hold on to his goal and concentrate as much of his time as possible to improving his basketball skills and strengthening his body. He also began to reach out to one of the coaches at the university he was targeting. The initial response was positive. Then nothing. During the silence, Daniel continued to practice. Finally, after reviewing video footage of his past performances on the basketball court, the assistant coach invited him to walk onto the team! In the years leading up to that moment, Daniel remained determined and continued to focus on the tasks required to make him a contender. His perseverance paid off.

Too many times, people quit right before their breakthrough. Circumstances change, people transition, priorities shift, and money dries up. Things really can begin to look bleak. It's during these times you must hold on tighter to your goal and remain focused. You must keep your goal in front of you, so you don't lose hope or forget about it. Often when you're reaching your breaking point, this is when you're closest to achieving your goal.

Because I often ask people, "What do you want?" my friend shared another part of Daniel's journey with me that's important to share with you. During these trying years for Daniel, my friend placed a large piece of paper on the ceiling over his bed to help him manage his thoughts. It was the first thing he saw in the morning when he awakened, and the last thing he saw at night before drifting off to sleep. This is what he saw:

He didn't lose sight of what it was he *wanted*—not what he *could* have, *thought* he could have, or *what others told him* he should want. When the circumstances became difficult, he was given a tool to help him to stay focused on his goal. By doing so, he earned a spot on the team.

Don't Allow Quitting to Be an Option

During Daniel's trial, I'm sure there were plenty of times when he wanted to give up and say, "Screw this!" I know I've had plenty of days when I wanted to quit working toward my goals. Isn't it funny how we can generate 100 reasons why we should quit on the tough days and, maybe, one reason why we shouldn't? Our justifications for throwing in the towel seem perfectly logical.

On those tough days, if you can only find one reason to keep going, let your reason be because you made a *promise* to yourself in the beginning that you would not quit. As the old saying goes, you told yourself, "Come hell or high water, I will not quit!" This means when you begin your journey, make this promise to yourself. Then you can be reminded of it when things get tough.

Along any journey, you may experience times when you need a break. That's okay. It's wise to periodically take a break to regroup and renew. Pursuing new goals is sexy and fun, and it's common to expend tremendous amounts of energy on it, then run out of gas in the midst of your efforts. If you try to force yourself to go on, likely you won't achieve the results you want. In writing this book, I didn't hesitate to step away from it when I felt like I had exhausted my brain power. I could tell when I needed a break because my writing was forced and I didn't like what I was seeing on paper. By stepping away for a few hours or days, it gave me time to clear my head so new ideas could come.

If your pursuit is an effort that can take years to achieve, certainly there will be times when you'll need to step away from it. If regrouping and refocusing takes a month or longer, don't beat yourself up—practice some self-compassion during this time. You'll feel renewed and come back stronger and better. Just make sure you return to your goal to continue on!

Celebrate!

Working to achieve any goal can be tough. If you're working on a goal that can extend over a period of time, it can be even tougher. One of the best ways you can serve yourself in a major pursuit is to celebrate when you achieve milestones along the way. Considering everything it often takes to achieve a major goal, you can easily become worn down by your efforts. Through the creation of small celebrations along the way, you boost your own motivation to finish.

The great news is you get to choose your milestones and celebrations! Whatever milestones you choose, pick celebrations that are special to you and motivate you to keep going. If you use the goal sheet I provided in Chapter Nine, a great way to incent your-self is to select specific places throughout the sheet for your mile-stones. Next, select a different type of celebration for each mile-stone—variety is always fun. The larger the milestone, the larger the celebration. If you achieve a key action step, a good celebra-tion may be temporarily breaking your diet by indulging in your favorite dessert (just once!). When you complete a strategy, you might treat yourself to a relaxing massage. If it's something that's meaningful for you and will incent you to move forward in your pursuits, it's not off-limits.

What's Next?

Identifying, planning for, and achieving goals is never easy, but the satisfaction you gain from your success is immeasurable. Once done, use the excitement, satisfaction, and confidence you feel to achieve an even bigger goal. If you continue to take this approach, you'll achieve much and enjoy many celebrations.

I leave you with these words to live by:

The road to victory is not straight. There is a curve called **Fear**, a loop called **Confusion**, speed bumps called **Struggle**, red lights called **Failure**, flats called **Layoffs**, and caution lights called **Ene-mies**. But, if you have a spare tire called **Determination**, an engine called **Consistency**, gasoline called **Creativity**, insurance called **Confidence**, and a driver called **Your Source**, you will make it to a place called **Success**.

Here's to your success.

Questions to Ponder

1. Discuss a goal you set out to achieve, but weren't able to complete? What caused the detour? How did the failure to complete the goal make you feel?

2. Describe a major goal you were able to complete? What roadblocks did you encounter? How did you press past them?

3. By setting your mindset to expect tough times in the beginning, how do you think this can help you as you move forward in pursuing your next goal?

4. For your next goal, what tough times can you expect now so you're prepared to face them if they show up?

5. Name some ways you can keep your goals in front of you so you don't lose sight of what you're pursuing and why?

6. List some small and large celebrations you can incorporate into the pursuit of your goals.

7.

About the Author

Bernie Frazier, SPHR is the Founder and President of CA-REERCompass, LLC, a speaking and career coaching firm based in St. Louis, MO. She also spent almost 25 years recruiting talent to six organizations across four industries, and led the Talent Acquisition function for four of those organizations, including one global team.

Bernie is a sought-after speaker, career strategist, job search, and recruiting expert. As a speaker, she has presented for numerous businesses and organizations. She has coached professionals from around the globe, from chief executive officers to individual contributors, on the fine art of career development and job search effectiveness.

Bernie holds a bachelor's degree in Marketing from Drake University in Des Moines, IA and is a Senior Professional in Human Resources. In her spare time, she volunteers as a Board

Member for It's Your Birthday, Inc., and teaches job skills classes for local nonprofit organizations.

To learn more about Bernie and CAREERCompass please visit her website at www.CAREERCompassLLC.com. You can also follow her on social media on her Facebook fan page, Twitter, LinkedIn, and YouTube.

Sample Values List

INSTRUCTIONS:

- Your Values are what is important to you in life. Knowing your Values helps you understand what drives you—what you enjoy, inspires you and would like more of. By **building a career and lifestyle around our values, we create a career and life that is more satisfying and meaningful** to us.
- Values change over time, and deepen as you understand yourself better—they are always moving. Your Values can also be situational—so what is true for you at work may not be true for you at home.
- Finally, the Values "List" below is ONLY to give you some ideas of example or sample values. We are each unique, so there will undoubtedly be words that are missing from this list, and different words that sum up your Value better. If so, feel free to add those words to the list below.

1.	Accomplishment	10.	Challenge
2.	Accuracy	11.	Collaboration
3.	Acknowledgement	12.	Colleagues
4.	Adventure	13.	Community
5.	Authenticity	14.	Compassion
6.	Balance	15.	Compensation
7.	Beauty	16.	Comradeship
8.	Boldness	17.	Confidence
9.	Calm	18.	Connectedness

19.	Contentment	48.	Helpfulness
20.	Contribution	49.	Honesty
21.	Cooperation	50.	Honour
22.	Courage	51.	Humour
23.	Creativity	52.	Idealism
24.	Curiosity	53.	Independence
25.	Determination	54.	Innovation
26.	Directness	55.	Integrity
27.	Discovery	56.	Intuition
28.	Ease	57.	Joy
29.	Effortlessness	58.	Kindness
30.	Empowerment	59.	Learning
31.	Enthusiasm	60.	Listening
32.	Environment	61.	Love
33.	Excellence	62.	Loyalty
34.	Fairness	63.	Open Dialogue
35.	Flexibility	64.	Optimism
36.	Focus	65.	Orderliness
37.	Forgiveness	66.	Participation
38.	Freedom	67.	Partnership
39.	Friendship	68.	Passion
40.	Fun	69.	Patience
41.	Generosity	70.	Peace
42.	Gentleness	71.	Presence
43.	Groundedness	72.	Productivity
44.	Growth	73.	Recognition
45.	Happiness	74.	Respect
46.	Harmony	75.	Resourcefulness
47.	Health	76.	Romance

77.	Safety	91.	Unity
78.	Self-Esteem	92.	Vitality
79.	Service	93.	Wisdom
80.	Simplicity	94.	Work Content
81.	Spirituality	95.	_____
82.	Spontaneity	96.	_____
83.	Supervisor	97.	_____
84.	Strength	98.	_____
85.	Tact	99.	_____
86.	Thankfulness	100.	_____
87.	Tolerance	101.	_____
88.	Tradition	102.	_____
89.	Trust	103.	_____
90.	Understanding		

Remember: When it comes to Values, there is no right or wrong—only who YOU are!

"Open your arms to change,
but don't let go of your values."
Dalai Lama

Your Success is in YOU!

For additional information about any of the following, please contact Info@CAREERCompassLLC.com or (314) 482-5650:

- Additional quantities of this book (quantity discounts may apply)
- Have Bernie speak to your organization or group
- Career coaching/strategy services
- Download a free, 19-page white paper, "7 Powerful Strategies to Navigate Your Next, Best Career Opportunity" from Bernie's website, www.CAREERCompassLLC.com.

For information about future products, virtual training, speaking events, and more tips for creating a fantastic career, "like" Bernie's Facebook fan page (Facebook.com/CAREERCompassLLC), and follow her on LinkedIn and Twitter(@BAFrazier).